Professional Etiquette for Writers

Professional Etiquette for Writers

William Brohaugh

 Cincinnati, Ohio

Library of Congress Cataloging-in-Publication Data

Brohaugh, William.
    Professional etiquette for writers.
    Bibliography: p.
    1. Authorship. 2. Authors and publishers. 3. Business etiquette. 4. Professional ethics. I. Title.
PN155.B76 1986   808'.02   86-23387
ISBN 0-89879-232-0

Dedication

The very existence of *Professional Etiquette for Writers* honors my parents, Earl and Hazel Brohaugh, whose standards of professionalism, precision, courtesy, persistence, and everyday fair play, lovingly and patiently instilled in an impatient young man, have allowed me to reach the position in life I hold now, and will be responsible for everything else I will ever accomplish. My parents take pride in what they do. I take pride in who they are, and who they have helped me to become.

This book is also for Sue, who hung in there.

Acknowledgments

Among the people who have helped me complete this book, directly or indirectly, are Susan Protter, Sharon Rudd, Thomas Clark, Diane Cleaver, Evan Marshall, Barbara Norville, Greg Daugherty, Carol Cartaino, Beth Franks, Howard Wells, and John Brady. Also, my gratitude to the editorial and production staffs at Writer's Digest Books, who worked so hard to get this book into your hands.

Thanks, too, to my mother, who bought me a 1920s manual typewriter sometime in the late '60s for ten dollars. When my word processor costing hundreds of times that threw in the electronic towel about halfway through this book, the fine old L.C. Smith & Corona "Silent" typewriter filled in without complaint. Mom, I owe you a ten-spot, and maybe a hug. (Turns out the computer problem was corrected with a bit of simple maintenance, and this book was eventually submitted electronically, via computer disk.)

But most of all, I must thank the hundreds of writers who have worked with me professionally and courteously over the years. They have taught me many, many lessons about grace and conscientiousness. Though my tales of unprofessionalism in this book might lead you to believe otherwise, the writers who are joys to work with far outnumber those whose manners must be polished a bit.

Contents

Introduction 1

1   Comedies of Manners, and the Seriousness of Manners 3

2   Attitude: The Foundation of Professional Etiquette 7

3   The Etiquette of Selling Your Work 11

4   Manners of the Mailbox 17

5   The Protocol of Patience 33

6   "Editor-quette": The Protocol of the Editor-Writer Relationship 41

7   Phone Etiquette: In the Manners of Speaking 57

8   In-Person Etiquette 67

9   Sources of Respect/Respect of Sources 77

10 The Most Important Words in the Professional Writer's Vocabulary 85

11 The Diplomacy of Disagreement: Arguments, Negotiations, and Complaints 89

12 The Bizarre World of "Rejecting" Rejection 103

13 The Only Person Who Absolutely Deserves Your Respect and Courtesy 111

14 A Brief Word on Personal Etiquette 115

15 A Final Word 117

Appendix: A Beginner's Quiz 119

Bibliography 123

Index 125

Professional Etiquette for Writers

Introduction

Like water and electricity, editors, agents, writers—everyone you'll ever come into professional contact with—seek the path of least resistance. Simply put, they just don't want to deal with unnecessary fuss and falderal.

Given the choice between two clients with equally good books, an agent will choose the one who is reliable, friendly, courteous, and professional over the one who's moody, argumentative, lackadaisical, and generally a pain. Given a similar choice between two contributors of equal writing skills, an editor will work with the one who queries professionally, doesn't waste the editor's time with long and chatty phone calls, doesn't try to hype his way into sales, and generally demonstrates respect and courtesy not only to the editor but also to his sources and to himself over the one who misses deadlines, submits single-spaced manuscripts covered with corrections, makes revisions reluctantly, and generally gives more respect to himself than to his writing or his readers.

As I said, these agents and editors will seek the path of least resistance while doing their jobs. This book points out that path, by advising you in the art of professionalism, of dealing day-to-day in the publishing business with diplomacy, manners, and dignity. This is not a guide to, for instance, sales techniques or interview strategies; instead, it is a guide to the etiquette of selling, and to the protocol of interviewing, and to the courtesies involved in other matters.

The instructions given here aren't intended to make the editor's life easier—though they will have that effect. They are intended to get results for *you*: more sales, better assignments, more money, better treatment. Make life just a little easier for editors and other people you work with by submitting articles promptly, by keeping them up-to-date on the progress of your work, by treating them with the

1

courtesy they demand and deserve—by, in sum, taking a little extra effort to reduce their workload. They'll respond by making a little extra effort to increase yours. As an agent once commented, "Everyone is so overworked today that when someone does treat you with courtesy, you really notice it and appreciate it."

I'm not trying to suggest that writers genuflect before editors and agents. Demonstrating manners and professionalism is not kowtowing. Writers can disagree with editors, negotiate with them, even argue with them—if they do it gracefully.

This book tells you how to do that. It explains how and when to assert yourself. And it identifies the courtesies and professional treatment you can expect from editors and others in the business, and what you can do if you don't receive them.

Welcome, then, to *Professional Etiquette for Writers*. Enjoy the book. I wish you luck and success with your writing career.

—*Bill Brohaugh*

I

Comedies of Manners, and the Seriousness of Manners

Not long ago, I received a letter I wish I could say was unusual. After I read it, I turned to the other *Writer's Digest* editors. "I have someone else for the list of Writers We'll Never Work With Again," I said, and announced the writer's name. Then I read the letter aloud.

The writer was asking for more money for an article we had assigned him. "I would like to work with *Writer's Digest*," he wrote, "but I write for a living not for self-satisfaction. Now don't get your dander up, just agree to pay me a bigger fee."

Compare that to another letter I received from a writer requesting more money. "We see eye to eye on everything else about the assignment, but I have a problem with your proposed fee, which is less than I am accustomed to receiving, and more to the point, less than the author of such a piece deserves. I am all too aware that, like all editors, you undoubtedly have budgetary constraints. However, I will need to contact and interview a number of editors, and for that amount of effort, I believe a higher price would be fairer."

The second writer got the extra money. The first didn't even get the assignment. Why? The second writer showed me that he was a professional. The first showed me that he could become a pain in the neck. Both were well within their rights to ask for what they thought they deserved. But the first writer was well outside the bounds of professional propriety in the way that he asked. I ignored the clumsy punctuation. I ignored the fact that elsewhere in his letter he had talked about "photocopys," "a leter" and "liable suits." Instead, I dwelled on "don't get your dander up." As it turned out, it was a self-fulfilling prophecy. My dander was indeed up. It needn't have been, if that writer had written to me as one professional to another, if he had—as the other writer had done—been polite, if he had kept his elbows off the table and chewed with his mouth closed and just plain minded his manners.

Call it protocol. Etiquette. Courtesy. Propriety. Diplomacy. *Manners.* All these add up to professionalism, to the mutual respect that must be at the center of business relationships of any kind—the relationship of writer with editor, of writer with agent, of writer with information source. As Elizabeth Crow, editor-in-chief of *Parents* magazine, has said, "Writers and editors need each other so much that it's sad when something comes between them."

"But," I've been asked, "isn't the *writing* what ultimately counts?" Yes, but to only one person: the reader. As an editor, I'm buying words, but I'm dealing with people. The reader may not care about anything beyond the words, as those are all he has contact with. But the editor must correspond with *people*, meet with *people*, negotiate with *people*. Yes, I've put up with my share of bull from writers because of the excellence of their writing, but if I can get the same quality of writing from someone else who handles himself as a professional, I will. With no hesitation.

Put it this way: There's a meat market near my house. The meats there are good, but I could get steaks and chops and baby back ribs of equal quality at any of half a dozen other markets in my neighborhood. Yet, I always return to this market, because they serve me with something beyond mere civility. They wait on you promptly and courteously. With a smile. Without bull (would make a tough steak). In so many senses, the writer is selling the editor something on a par with meats. The writer is selling a product. At times, a highly creative and artistic product, granted, but still a product. And in the sales biz, whether you're selling meats or words or cars or lawn mowers, there's no point in insulting, harassing, annoying, or offending the customer.

WARNING SIGNS

It's not just that editors get grumpy when they encounter obnoxiousness or unreasonableness or rudeness, because discourtesy works against the writer on a number of deeper levels. It does more than annoy; it signals amateurism. It signals trouble.

For example, when I run up against a discourteous writer, I ask, "If this writer treats me so rudely, how will she treat the people she meets when researching the story and conducting interviews? What gaffes will she commit in the name of my magazine? Can I afford to let her represent us?"

By the same token, breaches of protocol are symptoms of a general lack of knowledge of the publishing business. When, for example, a writer voices fear that I might steal his manuscript or idea, I react to more than the inherent insult. Anyone who has even a moderate familiarity with publishing knows that stealing is rare. Someone who dwells paranoically on the *possibility* of such stealing doesn't have even that moderate familiarity, and chances are slim that he has the skills to research and write publishable material.

And perhaps I'm reacting on an even deeper level. Someone who fears that I would steal material can't trust me or my publication, and what kind of person would degrade himself by offering services to someone or something he doesn't trust? He can't possibly respect himself.

Gaffes also destroy any possibility of editors taking you seriously. Editors shake their heads at such mistakes, and sometimes laugh at them and pass them around the office and put them in files and forget their authors' ideas. I recently received a manuscript that was accompanied by a recipe for barbeque sauce. The recipe, obviously, had nothing to do with the manuscript. I remember the submission clearly enough (perhaps because the recipe called for too little lemon juice), but I don't remember the idea the writer was trying to sell. I do recall that we didn't accept it, though.

That sort of unprofessionalism hurts. It hurts the careers of those who exhibit it, because they insert themselves on lists of writers who editors will never work with again. And—oddly, unfairly— it hurts *you*. The actions of your freelance colleagues can reflect on you, just as your actions reflect on them. Whenever you act professionally, you make it easier for editors to accord respect not only to you, but also to other writers. Whenever you act unprofessionally, on the other hand—if you offend editors, insult or infuriate or even just peeve them—they will pick up the next submission from the morning's mail a little more warily, half expecting to find more offenses. The next writer suffers, just as you suffer thanks to the actions of unprofessional writers who have preceded you.

The increasing number of book publishers who refuse to consider unsolicited submissions is evidence of this. So many of these publishers received one ridiculous, inappropriate submission too many, and decided to close their doors to unsolicited material. None of those submissions—none of the handwritten manuscripts or the historical tomes sent to science fiction houses or the stories typed single-spaced on both sides of the paper—none of them are your doing, but the door is as closed to you as it is to those who did submit those manuscripts. Don't allow other writers to suffer because of your gaffes. You owe it to your colleagues and to your very profession to act conscientiously, reasonably, and courteously whenever possible.

Is There Really an Editorial Blacklist?

Do editors have actual lists, posted on walls or stored within reach in drawers, headed "Writers We'll Never Work With Again"? No. But they *do* have good memories in such matters. I recently received a manuscript from someone whose name sounded familiar to me. It took me only a few moments to realize that "Hey, that's the writer from six years ago who. . . ." And they do share their experiences with their colleagues. "There are manners; there are courtesies," says Susan Protter, a New York agent. "This is a small business, and if you get a reputation as not behaving yourself, you're in trouble."

Happily, editors' memories are even better when it comes to writers who act professionally, courteously, considerately. Those are the writers they want to remember. And do.

2

Attitude:
The Foundation of
Professional Etiquette

There's a saying popular now in sports circles: *Stay within yourself.* That sums up a philosophy that applies to publishing circles as well: Know what you are capable of and what your goals are. Maintain humility. Don't force yourself to be what you're not. Be determined, but not obsessed. Develop a realistic, professional attitude.

Professionalism, when all is said and done, is a matter of taking your work seriously, but not taking yourself too seriously. Writing is fun and interesting. But it's also work. As writer Bil Gilbert once said, "Writing is tedious, but it's my line of work. Like a carpenter, there are some things that are tedious, but they're also fun because he knows how to do them. It's not glamorous; it's not being on the Johnny Carson show. It's being down in the damn basement worrying about the word *the*."

Professionalism is an overriding attitude that must come from within you. It's integral to who you are. It is not a posture you assume while trying to make it, and shed once success is at hand. Isaac Asimov, for instance, has published more than 300 books, and counting his magazine articles and short stories would probably take as long as it takes him to publish his next 300. When I assigned him to write an article for *Writer's Digest*, I offered him our standard kill fee—that is, a fee we'd pay even if we couldn't use the article. "Oh, no," he said. "I don't want a kill fee. If I fail to give you the article you want, I get nothing. I don't want to be paid for failure." Of course, writers deserve kill fees when they're appropriate, but Asimov's attitude toward the very concept of the kill fee demonstrates exemplary conscientiousness and, yes, courtesy to his editor, and ultimately to his readers.

As Asimov demonstrated, being a writer—even being a wildly successful writer—doesn't buy the right to ignore manners; it isn't a ticket to arrogance. I grant you that the work writers do almost demands an ego larger than that, say, of plumbers or stock brokers. They take pride in their work, certainly, but their investment of pride may not be the same as your investment of heart, of art. But becoming jealous of that investment and exercising your ego too much can stand in your way. Always remember the difference between demonstrating pride and becoming a prima donna.

MEGALOMANIACS NEED NOT APPLY

That pencil in your hand in no way entitles you to arrogance, to view yourself as a creative genius with rights not normally accorded to mortals. You *are* special. But, frankly, so is everyone involved in this special business. Creativity, therefore, is not a license for grandiosity. An inflated ego is a signal of trouble. Sharon Rudd, a *Writer's Digest* editor, gives an example of a writer she worked with during her days at a New York book publisher: "He claimed that he was a 'gifted writer' simply because his birthday was the same as Shakespeare's. His book was useful enough for what it was, but hardly a subject that no one had ever written about before. Yet, he predicted first that it would be a bestseller, then that it would sell a million copies, then that it would sell five million copies throughout the world. He called me every day, wanting to know about subsidiary rights sales (although he knew next to nothing about sub rights), expecting general encouragement and moral support, and, all around, taking up my time. It got to the point where one day he called me and sobbed on the phone, then the next day called and threatened me."

You may very well be a creative genius, and your genius will carry you far. Think how much farther it will carry you if you cooperate with people, and treat them with a businesslike, respectful attitude.

And how much farther still if you treat those around you with compassion, even kindness. We once bought a profile of Ray Bradbury, written by Tim Perrin, at about the same time I was asking Bradbury to write an original article for us. He agreed to write that article.

After we accepted Perrin's manuscript, Perrin sent a copy to Bradbury. When Bradbury received Perrin's piece, he called me.

"Have you read this profile?" Bradbury asked.

"Yes," I said.

"What did you think of it?"

"I liked it very much."

"Good. Why don't you use this instead of something by me?"

"Well," I said, "I don't see any problem in running them both. I don't see much potential for overlap."

"Oh, OK. I'll go ahead and write the article, then. I just didn't want to get in the way of this young writer."

That story exhibits compassion and kindness from a consummate professional, a man who truly *is* a genius, and it exhibits so much more: humility, self-confidence, respect for colleagues.

WRITER, READ THYSELF

Another implication of staying within yourself is understanding who "yourself" is. Understand your goals: don't waste your time or anyone else's pursuing projects that won't ultimately serve you. This, in a sense, is a matter of understanding your limitations. Or, as you've heard people say before, don't make any promises you can't keep. That point is best made by an exchange of letters I had with a writer who had queried me on an article topic; I didn't want anything on that specific subject, but thought he could do something related for us, and suggested that he tackle a different subject. His letter responding to my suggestion sums up the situation well. "Thank you for inviting me to submit a proposal on how to get big-city editors interested in heartland stories. I'd like to take you up on it, but I doubt that I'm qualified. As you recall, my original proposal was a story on how to bring information to the heartlands. Your idea is better than mine, but my background doesn't make me any more of an expert on that subject than other freelancers. I sell only an occasional story about a local, or heartland, subject to editors outside of my area. . . . So, although it was nice to be on the threshold of a *Writ-*

er's Digest assignment, I'll have to pass on your proposal. I'd rather come up with another query on a subject that I feel I can write intelligently about and with some authority."

My response: "You're a gentleman, sir, for bowing out for all the right reasons, and for letting me know why. I hope we'll be able to get together on a project sometime; it's always a pleasure to work with someone so conscientious."

You owe it to yourself and to the people who depend on you for excellent writing to be honest about what you can and can't accomplish, what you should and shouldn't pursue, where you are strong and where you are weak. This doesn't mean that you can't strive to do what you haven't accomplished before, that you should foreshorten your goals. It simply points to realism—optimistic realism—as an element of the honesty that should permeate any business relationship.

In sum, you want to be confident, but not unrealistic, not arrogant. You want to be enthusiastic, but not obnoxious. You want to prod and inspire, but not push. You want to promote yourself, but you don't want to deify yourself. Be realistic. Be humble. Be polite. Be yourself.

And remain within yourself.

3

The Etiquette of
Selling Your Work

Newhart, the TV comedy featuring Bob Newhart as successful how-to book writer Dick Louden, once broadcast an episode that tickled me as a viewer, but irked me as an editor. The plot is this: When a book Louden has written under the pseudonym of Dwight Schmidlap is rejected by his regular publisher, he vows to sell it elsewhere. In his marketing, he resorts to subterfuge: posing as a friend of a brother-in-law of a publisher. He resorts to skullduggery: giving his manuscript to a cleaning lady who has consented to sneak it into the publisher's office. He resorts to minor-league blackmail: threatening to expose a publisher with a source of Cuban cigars to customs officials if the publisher doesn't read the book.

We learn at the end of the show that Louden a/k/a Dwight Schmidlap sells the book. The minor-league blackmail worked.

Now, I'm not expecting complete adherence to reality in TV sitcoms. Still, as we watched I found myself grumbling to my wife, "Writers wouldn't resort to such ridiculous gambits."

And they wouldn't.

But they would resort to gambits almost as ridiculous.

And they have.

We laugh when Dick Louden poses as the publisher's brother-in-law's friend. Yet, the week before I saw that show, I received a particularly transparent attempt to win a biased reading from me, a letter that began, "One of your colleagues in the publishing business thought that the enclosed might work for you." The very vagueness alerted me, and the submission itself confirmed it: no colleague of mine—at least, not one that I'd ever want to work with again—would suggest that someone send me two pages of fantasy/fairy tale, typed in ALL CAPITAL LETTERS, no less.

And though I have no tales analogous to the cleaning-lady courier or the cheroot charade, I have no doubt that I could find more than one editor who does.

But what I really should have grumbled to my wife while we watched *Newhart* is: "No *professional* writers would resort to such ridiculous gambits." Gimmicks and gimcracks and gambits carry an implicit insult: "You as an editor are such a gullible rube that you will be mesmerized by pyrotechnics—nodding and saying yes and writing me a check while reflections of the sparks are still in your eyes." But editors usually see pyrotechnics for what they are: the flashes of bombs going off.

There are dangers in resorting to sales "ploys" that go beyond the potential of blowing up in your face, and they're all related to three myths about breaking into print:

It helps if you know someone in the business, even if it's a cleaning lady. Well, it doesn't hurt—a contact within the business can offer general information and advice, but it doesn't necessarily help, because editors seek to buy from writers who can supply what they need, not from friends and acquaintances.

You can clinch the sale just by getting the editor to notice you. This leads to writers using colored paper and enclosing gifts in submissions and using smiling-face stickers on outside envelopes. One writer once sent a box of chocolates—each chocolate in the shape of a deer—with each submission of her book on wildlife. These ploys gain you attention, all right, but it's the same sort of attention you might get had you slipped on a banana peel.

You can talk your way into a sale. You can't. Your writing can, but you can't. Therefore, don't try to sway editors and agents with cajolery.

Don't, for example, expect editors to be swayed by "expert" evaluations of your manuscript. Editors don't need, nor do they want, the opinion of your writing instructor, your next-door neighbor the English teacher, your writer friend, or your sister who reads the magazine and says this is better than anything it has ever print-ed. If editors need second opinions, they have other editors and writers—people associated with their publications and familiar with their needs—to turn to. Including testimonials from your peers im-plies that you think the editor is a bit dim and needs some prodding (or that she believes that *it helps to know someone in the business*—see above). Worse yet, those testimonials can signal a lack of confidence in the manuscript itself. Says writer Elana Lore, who has worked as an editor at *Ellery Queen's Mystery Magazine* and *Sylvia Porter's Personal Finance* magazine: "The absolute kiss of death for a manuscript, for most editors, is delivered even before the first page of the manu-script is read. A cover note that says 'my family and friends think this is the best story I've written' usually means it's dreadful, even when this phrase is penned by successful authors. For some reason, writers seem compelled to say this when they have grievous doubts about the quality of a particular piece."

Similarly, don't expect anyone to be swayed by *your* opinion; don't tell editors or agents how good the work is. Let the work itself say that. Boasting does nothing but confirm the existence of your ego, and the very fact that you have offered your work for inspec-tion, criticism, and possible acceptance already demonstrates that. And don't explain how many millions the manuscript will make for the publisher, or how many millions of people need what you have written. If there are millions or hundreds of thousands or whatever of any sort within the manuscript's pages, editors are better equipped to see them there than you are. There is an exception to this, as explained by one editor: "When pitching a book idea, it can be a sales point if there is a large pre-existing market, such as musi-cians, teenage girls, retirees, or nature lovers, that the writer can point to as prospective buyers. This needs to be semi-scientific, edu-cated guesswork—use statistics, sales figures, surveys, etc.—but the editor usually really appreciates the writer's input here, because this information will be needed when the book is presented to the editorial board for possible publication. On the other hand, saying that 'Everyone will read it' is not in the writer's best interest, because it shows a complete lack of awareness of *targeting the market*."

In general, put your faith in the quality of the book, not in its commerciality, and put it there quietly, in the words of the manu-script, not in unsubstantiated hype in the cover letter or sales pitch. "If writers are ecstatic about the progress of their work," says agent

Susan Protter, "it's probably not their best work. They are probably drunk on the work."

Don't tell people you're submitting to how good *they* are. In other words, don't resort to hollow flattery. Solid flattery isn't all that effective, either, though *informed* compliments or other sorts of comments do demonstrate to editors that you're familiar with their publications. For example, a query letter for a roundup piece might say: "I propose to structure the article along the lines of the roundup pieces you printed in the February and June issues last year. The clear presentation of those pieces would suit my article well." That demonstrates that you have studied the publication.

Also related: Don't tell anyone how good *you* are. Never take the attitude that you're doing editors or agents a favor by gracing them with your work. Whether or not you are indeed doing them a favor—in so many senses you are doing just that—is not at issue here. Your attitude is at issue. Don't write this letter, which I've seen a surprising number of times, each with similar wording: "I notice that you don't run much humor in your magazine, so I thought I'd give you a chance at the enclosed so you can spice the publication up a little." As an editor, I want to know how you'll fit in with the rest of my writers and contribute to the "personality" of the magazine; I don't want to hear plans for single-handedly upgrading the quality of my publication. (You're really in trouble if you write the above letter and the magazine *does* publish humor, or whatever.)

Don't dare editors to publish your submission. Professional relationships aren't built around challenges. Pleading doesn't do much good, either. It demeans both you and the relationships you propose to establish. It places a lot of tension on matters, as well, as agent Don Maass points out. In a list of beginners' mistakes, he includes the writer's professing "extreme financial need, especially self-inflicted (as with the corporate executive who has given up a $100,000-a-year job to write—yes, this really happens!). I cannot do my job properly when the author is sitting by the phone, hand on receiver, waiting to learn whether he will have a check by dinner time. It's not the pressure that bugs me, but that I must accept the first and easiest offer I can get."

Pressure does bug other publishing professionals, though. Don't nag about your submissions. And don't set deadlines—"I'll expect to hear from you within ten business days." As one editor I've worked with says, "People with garbage seem to put the pressure on." Lacking faith in the quality of the work, these writers hound the editor for a response, and they resort to hard sell and fast talk in trying to make the sale. "Tactics like that increase the chance of getting a *no*," says the editor, for these reasons:

1. Pressure is itself often obnoxious and rude.

2. The editor suspects that more energy is being spent on the pitch than on the writing. The editor is often right.

3. The faster an answer is made, the greater the chance that the answer will be *no*. The *yes*es always take a long time, especially in book publishing, where so many *yes*es, from editors and marketing people and others, must be gathered before the book is finally accepted. If you press editors for answers, they will more often than not respond with a safe *no* rather than a risky *yes*. An example comes from Barbara Norville, who has worked as an editor at several major publishers. She accepted a first novel by a writer whose books would eventually become award-winning bestsellers. "He had no agent, so I wrote him with the usual first-novel terms. A couple of days later, he phoned me and said, 'That sounds fine, but let me get back to you.' A couple more days passed and he phoned again. Apparently he had spent those days phoning paperback houses and got a nibble from one of them. So, naturally, he wanted his advance boosted right then and there. I stood firm and he accepted and the rest is history. But history you don't know about with first authors and I was not pleased with his pushiness. It was such inept razzledazzle. Had he continued pushing, I would have dropped him."

THE WHOLE TRUTH,
AND NOTHING OF THE UNTRUTH

Never, never resort to lies, half-truths, untruths, implied lies, or flexed truth to catch an editor's eye or get an assignment. Be honest. We once assigned a piece to a writer: he was to cover a certain type of sporting magazine, after having told us that there were fifteen such magazines then being published. When his article came in, he listed five magazines, produced by only three different publishers. We had to reject the piece; he could have saved the trouble of writing had he given us the full truth to begin with.

Also, don't tease editors in queries: "If you want to find out more, you'll just have to give me the assignment," or the book contract, or whatever. I've seen many queries rejected because the writer was, in the language of the card table, holding the cards too close to his chest. This isn't a poker game. Secretiveness and bluffing will get you nowhere. Your sales pitch should be self-contained; the editor should be able to decide based on what you present then and there.

But don't present too much. Some writers will present six or seven ideas in a single letter, and ask the editor to choose one. This has the feel of a basement clearance sale.

And threats to send the submission to a competitor will be laughed at heartily.

SUCCESSFUL SALES TACTICS

Here are a few sales gambits that *do* work:

Present yourself confidently. Never apologize when submitting material. Editors and agents daily receive letters saying, in effect, "You probably won't like this, but I thought I'd take a shot anyway." And that's a blatant symptom of lacking self-confidence. Some symptoms are more subtle: not having the courage to put that manuscript in the mail in the first place, for example.

Be honest and aboveboard on all dealings. If your query has been sent to other editors at the same time, admit it (I explain why in the next chapter). If you have no publishing credits, don't imply that you do. If you can't deliver the manuscript you're proposing to write, don't propose it in the first place.

Keep your sense of humor. If writing can't be enjoyable, why do it? Other jobs are easier and better-paying, and they place less stress on you and your ego. Enjoy yourself.

Exercise dedication and perseverance. One of my favorite stories of persistence involves a writer who kept circulating his book manuscript for years. Twenty-five years of submission finally paid off, and the book was published. For a quarter of a century, that writer did not give up. In terms of etiquette, that concept of dedication translates to follow-through, to keeping your promises. Accepting an assignment from an editor is making a promise. You must be true not only to your words, but also to your word.

In all, be honest, straightforward and controlled in your sales pitch. Sell manuscripts, not Brooklyn Bridges.

Manners
of the Mailbox

Many people in the publishing business will know your talent only by what you put on paper, and will know *you* only by what you put in the mail. Therefore, an important part of minding your p's and q's lies in minding letters of an entirely different sort: your queries, your submissions, your cover letters, and other types of business correspondence.

Courtesy in correspondence begins at the very top of the first page of a letter, whether a query, a letter covering a manuscript submission, a complaint letter, whatever. Make sure your name and address appear there. I've received dozens of queries that revealed the author's name *after* the "Sincerely yours." Can you imagine someone you've never met talking to you for fifteen minutes at a party and then introducing himself just before walking away?

Similarly, make sure the *operative* address—that is, your mailing address—appears on the first page. If you want correspondence sent to your home, don't use stationery from your place of business. Like every other editor, when I reply to a letter, I look at the top of the first page for an address. Not too long ago, a writer chastised me for sending letters to the school where she taught. Her home address, she assured me, was easy to find in her letters. Easy to find, yes, once she told me where it was: *after* the signoff. Not the first place I normally look for my correspondents' addresses.

As a matter of fact, you should always use letterhead that applies only to the business at hand. At *Writer's Digest*, we regularly receive queries identifying writers as doctors or lawyers. That would be OK if we published more medical and legal articles. Finding an envelope with "Attorneys at Law" in the return address always scares me for a moment: I wonder whether someone is bringing suit against me or my magazine. "M.D." return addresses make me wonder if I'm sick and don't know it. Letters with the word "Plumbing" in the letterhead have me wondering why out-of-state pipe jockeys are billing me.

On the other hand, if your professional letterhead does apply to the business at hand, by all means, use it. Doctors submitting medical pieces to general interest magazines, plumbers submitting how-to pieces to trade journals, editors submitting insider's reports to *Writer's Digest*—all have every right to use the letterhead that they have earned to establish their credibility and gain my attention.

LETTER PERFECT

Next, let's consider the letter's salutation. A sales rule dictates that you address a letter to a specific person. People respond to the respect implied by your using their names. They don't respond to "Dear Sir or Madam," which is the correspondence equivalent of "Hey you!" They also don't go much for "Greetings" or "Dear Editor" or the like. These are more polite than "Hey you," yet they communicate the same thing: laziness on your part. Writers who can't get up the ambition to find out my name, I think when I see such salutations, certainly won't get up the gumption to dig out the information I'll need in any articles they write for us.

Then there are the writers who just don't seem to be paying attention. They will type in the name—first, middle, and last—and address of the person they're writing to, and then type "Dear Agent" or, worse yet, "Dear Sir or Madam" when the name that should appear is six lines above.

Address your letters, on first contact, to a Mr. or a Ms. If a female correspondent identifies herself as a Mrs. when she signs her letter, address her as Mrs. (as in, for example, Mrs. Sue Smith—*never* Mrs. Thomas Smith). If you are uncomfortable with using the salutation Ms., as some people are, simply use the entire name: "Dear Patricia Smith." That's also a good technique when you're not sure of the sex of your correspondent. Better to play it safe with "Dear Pat

Smith" than to write "Dear Ms. Smith" only to find out that Pat has a handlebar mustache you could steer a bicycle with. Another way around that problem is to call the publisher and ask the receptionist if Pat is a man or a woman.

I personally don't care for "Dear Editor Brohaugh" as a salutation. It seems forced and contrived, a flimsy attempt at elevation or aggrandizement. Other editors I've talked to don't object, though, so the choice of using that style of salutation is up to you.

Follow standard business format in the body of the letter: single-spacing, double-spacing between paragraphs, starting the first line of each paragraph at the left-hand margin (if you follow modern style) or indenting it (if you follow traditional style).

The letter should allow the editor flexibility to respond to it in her own manner—and by that I mean that if she wants to write back to you, she can use the self-addressed, stamped envelope (SASE) you have provided (I'll discuss the SASE in detail in a moment). Or, if she wants to call you, she can use the phone number you have thoughtfully provided at the top of page 1. Wait for her to use one of those two mechanisms. A letter is not the first punch in a left-right combination: don't tag letters with lines like, "I will call you in two weeks to discuss this with you."

Whenever possible, cover one topic per piece of correspondence. For example, questions to a magazine editor about 1) the focus of the article you're writing, 2) why your subscription has lapsed, and 3) the editor's interest in a new article idea should each appear in a separate letter (although all three letters can be sent in the same envelope). Be courteous, and make it convenient for the editor to deal with each matter individually. There are exceptions, of course. If one person can handle the various matters, you can go ahead and cover all the topics in a single letter. But if more than one person must respond to you—a copy editor, a content editor, someone from the accounting department—devote a single piece of paper to each topic.

Actually, this is the better way to go overall, for two reasons: First, you probably won't be able to tell whether one person can deal with each item. Second, even if one person *can* handle each, he might not be able to deal with them all at once. Using separate sheets of paper guarantees separate handling—and helps preclude one or more items being overlooked.

At the end of the letter, sign off with your phrase of choice: Sincerely, or Cordially, or Yours, or Best. Just be careful about being cute (Hoping you have a nice day), or, if you're writing about a problem or complaint, snide (Yours, but you haven't bought me yet).

Don't forget to sign the letter. When I sold my first short story years ago, the acceptance letter was unsigned. I wondered for a moment if the acceptance were some kind of joke. (In a strange sort of way, it became a joke. The unsigned editor left, the magazine folded, my story never saw print. . . .)

Next, we turn over the final page of the letter to find the submission itself (or at least we hope to turn the page—don't be tempted to place such short submissions as fillers and poems on the same sheet as the cover letter). Send only neatly typed letters and manuscripts. That's more than smart marketing; it also demonstrates that you respect yourself and your work, that you respect the person receiving the letter or manuscript, and that you're extending a courtesy to the person who must read what you have written. That person reads constantly, and his or her eyes don't need extra work. Consider, too, that more than one person handles letters and manuscripts. The typical manuscript page, for instance, might be reviewed by one or more editors, scrutinized multiple times by a copy editor, reviewed by a designer (in the case of a book manuscript), followed closely by a typesetter, and compared to a typeset galley by one or more proofreaders. That's why when a writer asks me if it's OK to use dot-matrix printing on a manuscript because it's faster and easier, I reply, "For you, it is." For me, and for everyone else who will handle that manuscript, the less-than-crisp type adds work and strain to the job.

Photocopies should be sharp and legible. And the manuscript shouldn't be marred with too many hand-written corrections. Note that I said "too many"; a few are allowed, but if you have more than two on a page, you might consider retyping the page. If you're submitting material on assignment, or if you work regularly with an editor (writing a column for him, for instance), you can get away with more such hand-written corrections, but never allow yourself to get sloppy.

Follow these manuscript-preparation guidelines to give the manuscript a professional look:

- Double-space it for ease of reading, and to allow room to mark insertions and copy-editing symbols.

- Use one side of the paper for ease of handling (especially in the age of the photocopier).

- Leave the top third of the first page blank to allow the editor to jot in headlines and such.

- Use one-inch margins on the top, right, and bottom, and an inch and a half on the left margin to allow room to mark in copy-editing and typesetting symbols.

- Don't use erasable bond; it sticks to everyone's fingers.

- Submit manuscripts with their pages free. Paper clips present no problems, but don't staple the manuscript or place it in a binder. If you use computer fanfold paper (which you should do only if it is of a good weight and the perforations are discreet), separate the pages before you send them. One of the editors I work with growls at writers who don't: "Separate the sheets. Why should I have to do your work for you?" This point is especially true for book manuscripts, where hundreds of pages must be separated.

These "requirements," by the way, weren't created arbitrarily. They have evolved because they reduce the work of the editors and typesetters who deal with manuscripts. When you ignore these requirements, you are not only demonstrating lack of knowledge of industry standards, but also rudely refusing to extend common, expected courtesies to those you deal with.

THE ENVELOPE, PLEASE

Now, let's return to the envelope the correspondence came in. Use standard business-size stationery: #10 envelopes for letters, 9x12 envelopes for manuscripts of more than five pages (don't force the recipient to fight with six or seven pages folded into a #10), standard mailers (mailing boxes and bags are available at office-supply stores) for book-length submissions. Use fresh envelopes; don't recycle your used ones. We get frequent submissions from a writer who salvages his SASEs by taping a rectangle of paper over the canceled stamps and the return address. The envelope, having braved numerous postal service handlings, is battered, and the flap is a museum collection that might be titled "Tape From Editors' Desks Across the Country." Each of his submissions is difficult to handle, and looks silly. Take old envelopes to a paper recycling center if you're environmentally minded; don't toss the reused envelopes into the mailbox. It's about as bad as wearing a rumpled suit to a job interview.

Don't wear someone else's suit to the interview, either. I once received a query in an envelope that looked normal enough on the outside, except that an address label covered some printing underneath. When I opened the envelope, I first saw not a query, not a manuscript, but "Checking Deposit-by-Mail" instructions printed on the flap. I've also received queries in stationery envelopes from hotels, motels, ski shops, and airlines. Thrift is one thing; I believe in saving money whenever possible. Parsimony is another; I hesitate to work with these writers because I wonder where else their cheapness will surface: will they send similar envelopes to information sources, supposedly with our blessing, for instance? Or will they choose counting pennies over making the long-distance calls for information that could add depth to their manuscripts?

And definitely don't wear your *pajamas* to the job interview. I've received queries in envelopes adorned with drawings of flowers, cute forest animals, and fascinating geometric patterns. Colorful, but counterproductive. I knew of a writer who used nothing but one-cent stamps on his submission envelopes, which left little room for the address. Don't try to make your outside envelope stand out from its brethren in the slush pile. Such tactics only make editors roll their eyes and say, "Oh, come on." These are the devices of the Dwight Schmidlap character I discussed in Chapter 3.

Nothing Personal

Similarly, when writing to me, don't mark *Personal* on the outside unless you're my mom, my sister-in-law, a long-lost college buddy, or Steve Jenson, who owes me five dollars. Actually, I shouldn't sound so cranky on this point. There are numerous occasions when a personal note is appropriate. You've met an agent at a conference and want to thank her for chatting with you, say, or it's the holiday season and you want to send a card to an editor you've worked with a couple of times. Such personal correspondence is acceptable, and should certainly be identified as being personal.

What miffs me, though, are those writers who hope to slip correspondence past the first readers who screen all the mail and get my attention by tricking me into thinking that Steve has finally come through with the five bucks, and I open the so-called "personal" letter to find a query from someone I've never met. This is business; keep it on that level.

The same goes for *Confidential*. Mark correspondence thus only if it's imperative that only the addressee see it. Not many requests for writer's guidelines, for instance, are *really* confidential.

Ditto for anything else you might jot or stamp on the outside envelope just to attract attention, including *urgent*, *important*, and *immediate response requested*. On the other hand, you can and should label the outside envelope with phrases that will aid in routing your correspondence. If the letter really is personal or confidential, label it as such. If it's a query, a letter to the editor, an information request, a manuscript or information that the editor has asked for, or an urgent piece of business (it's best if the editor has determined its urgency—if he has, for instance, asked for a new lead ASAP), jot "Query," "Letter to the Editor," "Information Request," "Requested Information," "Requested Manuscript," or "Urgent—Deadline Material" on the outside.

Include your name and address on the outside envelope—especially important if you're sending something the editor is expecting. Type it, or have personalized envelopes printed. Gummed labels with your name on them should be reserved for the outside of Christmas cards. (And it may be a personal peeve, but return addresses printed on the back of the envelope irk me.)

Make sure the envelope is secured—that the flap has been properly glued down. Secure it, but don't fortify it. Don't cover every visible seam with so much duct tape that the editor must use a chainsaw to rescue the manuscript within.

Postpaid Rudeness

Finally, use your own envelopes; conduct correspondence on your nickel. Many magazine publishers use postpaid business reply envelopes for their customers' convenience. Subscribers, for instance, can pop their order forms and checks into such envelopes and return them to the publisher at no cost to them. If you should discover such an envelope, perhaps in a direct-mail solicitation (what some of you call "junk mail"), *don't* use it to submit a query and expect it to a) be routed to the right department and b) receive anything less than contempt from the editor. I've seen writers go so far as to glue business reply envelopes to the outside of packages of books, and send them in. The post office sees the postal permit number, dutifully jots the number down or whatever it does, and delivers the package to us—at our cost. This parsimonious way of saving a few stamps is one step below calling in phone queries collect.

Pack It Up

If you're inserting more than one sheet of paper into a letter-sized envelope, lay all sheets together and *then* fold them all, together. This is known as "nesting" the materials. Don't fold each sheet individually and slip them into the envelope; these will flop out of an open envelope and all over the recipient's desk like fish flopping out of an overturned net.

Submit everything pertaining to the submission in one package, if possible: manuscript, sidebars, artwork, and so on. If you send each under separate cover, you risk confusing the editor at best, and getting the material separated at worst. A particularly important warning: don't send a draft one day, and follow up with a revision two days later.

On the other hand, don't include too much in the package. Send only the materials that pertain to the submission. Don't send photocopies of your research, the outtakes and the false-start drafts, or alternative leads or endings, and then ask the editor to winnow through and select what works best. Send only the polished gold, not the ore you mined in looking for it. Book editors and agents, in particular, end up seeing thousands of pages of manuscript from writers asking the editors to select the best 250 pages. Demonstrate confidence in your work, and respect for your editor's time, by submitting what you know is the best you can do.

Before you put anything in the mail, copy it, and file the copy. There's little more embarrassing than writing a letter that says (as I've received): "Thanks for the assignment, but I didn't keep a copy of my query on hand. Could you send me a copy so I know what I told you I'd write for you?"

THE SASE

One of the basic tools of etiquette in dealing with anyone in this business is the SASE, the self-addressed, stamped envelope. One of my favorite SASE stories involves the note we received not long ago: "Can you tell me what SASE means? I've enclosed a self-addressed, stamped envelope for your reply." At least she was trying. My least favorite story involves a writer who, in response to our stated instructions to enclose SASE with submissions, wrote the word *SASE* all over her query letter. I still haven't figured that one out.

Whether you're submitting a query, submitting a manuscript, or asking a question of the editor, enclose that important SASE, for these reasons.

- It's a courtesy, pure and simple.

- It speeds response. Much simpler for an editor to jot a reply and pop it back into the SASE than to type up another envelope.

- It increases the chance of response. Recognizing the courtesy, the editor will be more inclined to answer your letter.

- It guarantees that the response will get where it's supposed to go. Better you type the address rather than someone who doesn't know it so well, and could mistype it.

Some people rebel against the SASE for two reasons: 1) It invites rejection. My response: *Not including it invites being ignored.* 2) The editor should bear part of the cost of this business correspondence. My response: *The editor didn't invite your submission*—if he did, that's a different matter. But an unsolicited submission without SASE is like an insurance agent calling you collect to peddle a policy. Look at it this way: suppose the circulation department of my magazine mails you an offer to subscribe. We enclose a sales pitch *and* a postpaid envelope to facilitate your reply, to make replying convenient for you. We are trying to sell you, the customer, a product. Now, when you're querying me, I become the customer, and you are trying to sell me a product. Enclose the sales pitch. Enclose the vehicle for easy, convenient reply.

As I said, the SASE policy changes if the editor has invited the submission. (A personal invitation is necessary; a listing in *Writer's Market* isn't an invitation, precisely.) If I called you on the phone and asked you if you could submit a couple of poems for our Writing Life page, I wouldn't expect you to enclose SASE.

Similarly, manuscripts written on assignment—making an assignment is, in a practical sense, the same as extending a business invitation—needn't be accompanied by SASE.

Always enclose SASE when sending material unsolicited to an agent, and when first submitting solicited material for review. But when the agent takes you on as a client, you aren't expected to enclose return postage with each new project you send to the agent.

Don't enclose SASE with a manuscript you have revised at the editor's invitation, unless you were asked to submit the revision on spec.

Anything you do regularly requires no SASE. For example, if you're writing a column for a magazine, a regular feature for a syndicate, or a series of books for a publisher. That advice also applies when you have become a "regular" for an editor, even if you don't write a column or such. By that I mean that if an editor has bought five or so pieces from you, and the relationship between the two of you looks solid, you can safely discontinue sending SASE with queries—if you want to.

When in doubt, enclose SASE. Some writers I know never include SASEs in their correspondence. Others go to the other extreme, and always include SASE, no matter the level of their relationship with a particular editor. Given a choice between the two, I'll work with the latter.

With word processors now common, meaning that the manuscript exists on disk and copies can be produced easily, writers often submit manuscripts with instructions that the editor should simply throw the manuscript away if it is rejected. No SASE is needed in this case. Clearly state those instructions to pitch the manuscript; don't make the editor guess about what you want.

One Size Fits All?

Your SASE should be large enough to allow the materials you have sent to be easily inserted and returned. Editors have told me— no kidding—of writers who have submitted book-length manuscripts along with SASEs suitable only for Christmas cards. Me, I've received any number of manuscripts submitted in 9x12 envelopes accompanied by #10 SASEs. It pains me to fold the previously un-wrinkled sheets so that I can fit them into the #10, but I do it any-way. A disfigured return is better than no return at all, and, besides, the writer has, in essence, asked that I fold the submission by en-closing a too-small SASE.

With book submissions, some publishers will allow you to en-close only the return postage, omitting an outer return envelope, if the manuscript was submitted in a box or mailer that will protect it. Paper-clip the postage to a mailing label with your name and ad-dress on it. The editor can then slip the manuscript into one of the publisher's envelopes, and attach the label and the postage to the outside. Other publishers prefer that you include the return enve-lope, saying that loose postage is too easily lost. When in doubt, in-clude the return envelope.

Some writers will include a #10 SASE for a letter from an editor, and a larger SASE for the manuscript's return, usually by less-expensive fourth-class mail.

THE MULTIPLE SUBMISSION

Eagerness, concern for efficiency, and sometimes plain old impa-tience lead some writers to make what's known as a multiple sub-mission or a simultaneous submission. That is, they duplicate their manuscripts, then send them to a number of editors at once. This can indeed be an efficient marketing method: you don't have to wait as some editor dawdles over your manuscript before getting it to the next potential buyer. A book manuscript that might have taken—let's face it—years to make the rounds of, say, twenty-five publish-ers could make its way to those same twenty-five in a matter of days. This is especially important when the manuscript is hot—that is, when it's timely. A biography of an entertainer who has just hit the big time is an example of a hot manuscript.

This practice is becoming increasingly common, but its accept-ance among editors and agents isn't increasing nearly as quickly. Many want to consider only submissions that aren't at that moment being considered anywhere else. They want to feel that they have been accorded the privilege of seeing the manuscript exclusively, and they don't want to be pressured into making a decision before a competing editor or agent beats them to it.

Others don't care.

"Multiples," as they're called, are generally better accepted in book publishing than magazine publishing, because everyone acknowledges that the response time is longer with book submissions than with magazines. In fact, with truly timely books, multiple submission is practically a *must*. Let's return to that example of the entertainer who has just hit. This is a hot topic, because it's in danger of cooling quickly. The entertainer might fade within a year, and with her, the public's interest in buying a book about her. That's the best definition of "hot" that I've heard: Hot is something that can cool. As book topics, therefore, sex and self-help are not hot topics, as there's no danger of readers losing interest in them.

Still, no matter the circumstances, each editor holds his own opinion of the practice. To find out which editors do and don't accept simultaneous submissions, consult *Writer's Market*.

If you decide to submit your manuscript to more than one editor at the same time, lay your cards on the table. Tell each editor that the submission before her is being considered by others. The first reason to do this is to protect yourself in the unlikely, stuff-dreams-are-made-of event that two or more editors express interest. You can then accept one offer, and decline the others with a simple statement that the manuscript is no longer available.

Suppose that does happen? Which offer do you accept? The one that you want to. Go with the best-paying market, or the most prestigious market, or the one that's going to treat you best. (I recently accepted an article that had been submitted to me over the transom, only to find out—when the author wrote back to decline—that the article had been a simultaneous submission that another editor was interested in. The author had accepted the other offer not because of money—I was offering more—and not because of the size of the publication—mine had the wider readership—but because the other editor's letter of acceptance had been dated before mine. That seems to be a bit *too* considerate to the buyer.)

Do not accept both offers, or you might receive a letter like the one I was forced to write after opening the February issue of a competing magazine to find the very same article I had just published in *my* February issue: "We were surprised and distressed to find your article in *two* magazines. Such duplicate marketing of articles, unless all editors involved know precisely what's going on, is unfair and unwise, particularly if the magazines involved are national and share a certain part of their audiences. By marketing the same article to different magazines without informing editors of what's going on, you risk alienating and angering those editors. Be assured that you have a group of alienated and angered editors here."

That double sale, by the way, was not only unprofessional, but also illegal. As I told the writer, "Each magazine bought first serial rights to the article. We're hard-pressed to figure out which magazine got what it paid for." This is not to say that you can't sell an article more than once, if you sell different sorts of rights, and if everyone is apprised of the sales. You can, legally and ethically, sell a manuscript to one magazine, and then approach another and offer reprint rights. The author above could have done that.

Stay away from multiple submissions when the potential markets are few, and covering them one at a time won't take all that long. For example, I'm leery of simultaneous submissions to *Writer's Digest*, because we have but one major competitor; how much time does a writer save by hitting all two of us at once? What's more, I must ask myself how much is missing from the query because the writer hasn't tailored it to our special needs, which are quite a bit different from those of our competitor.

Turn to simultaneous submissions only when they serve the manuscript and its marketing, not when it serves your impatience. As I said, timely material can legitimately be submitted simultaneously. And a manuscript sent to noncompeting markets might as well be submitted to all at once. By noncompeting markets, I mean those that don't vie for the same readers. This applies only to the magazine world; every book publisher is, basically, in competition with every other.

For example, a general interest piece on some upcoming social trend—severe declines in television-watching, for instance—might fit the Sunday magazine of a Boston newspaper and the features section of an Albuquerque paper equally well. The piece could appear in both places, and in other newspapers as well, without a single reader seeing it more than once. Therefore, the editors involved can hardly balk at your submitting that piece simultaneously. Still, it's wise to explain that the piece is being reviewed by other editors across the country. No need to state exactly who has it, but do stress that the readerships of the papers reviewing the piece don't overlap. Other examples of noncompeting publications include trade magazines (a trade published for restaurant owners and one for gift-shop operators might be equally interested in a piece about improved bookkeeping methods), and religious publications (an uplifting nondenominational piece might find as comfortable a home in a Presbyterian weekly as in a Catholic monthly).

Custom-Made Queries

If you are submitting multiple queries, have the courtesy to write letters tailored to their recipients. It's that personalized touch that many editors and agents miss when they receive mass-produced queries and manuscript submissions. "I'm looking for some sense of personality in a query," says one agent, "not a form copied out of a book. I'm looking for creativity," and creativity doesn't surface in, say, a query letter that is typed over and over, with no change save the person each copy is addressed to. Besides, editors want material and ideas that address their readers specifically; they shun material and ideas that haven't been so tailored.

The multiple-submission-as-gaffe is made much easier by today's technology. "Half of the writers have word processors these days, and they commit a lot of blunders with their multiple queries," says the agent. "They do so much multiple querying that agents these days ask each other, 'Did you get that one?' Writers don't understand that a multiple query just doesn't get the same kind of consideration." (One editor has noted that the writers who crank out production-line queries are the same ones who neglect to sign them.)

Of course, you don't need a word processor to commit the production-line gaffe; I've seen some writers use pre-computer-chip ingenuity to write the body of the letter, photocopy it, then type in the recipient's address and a "personalized" salutation onto the photocopy. This is as obvious as it is tacky.

Mass production can lead to another problem: slipping the wrong materials into the envelope. "We've often gotten a competitor's copy of a query (the one addressed to Mrs. so-and-so at Simon & Schuster or Mr. so-and-so at St. Martin's) in our envelope," an editor once complained to me. That's about the same as an automobile production line jamming a front-wheel-drive engine into a rear-wheel-drive car.

Remember that if you send many queries on the same topic to different magazines with the intent of writing a different article for each publication, you really aren't making a multiple submission. A multiple is when the final product is substantially the same. If I were to send this chapter to several editors, that would be considered a multiple. But if I were to query those same editors about articles discussing use of the mails, each article written specifically for that editor's audience, I am submitting a series of separate articles. For example, I might want to address the dangers of "production-line" letter-writing for a computer magazine, the etiquette of addressing letters for a magazine for secretaries, and general manuscript-preparation techniques for a writing magazine. I don't have to tell anybody that I'm querying those three publications at the same time, since I'm not really in danger of selling the same thing to more than one editor.

P.S.

You don't, of course, have to follow these guidelines to the, excuse me, letter. The International Bureau of Weights and Measures has issued no standards for manuscript-preparation, for how to address envelopes, for how to address the person you're writing. Neatness, legibility, and common sense are the overriding concerns here. You must remember that in most cases editors will form their first impression of you by what you present to them in the mail.

Make that impression a good one.

5

The Protocol of Patience

I'm not given to quoting fortune cookies, but a friend of mine recently got a fortune that is particularly apt. "Manners require time. Nothing is more vulgar than haste."

Haste is at the core of a variety of etiquette "sins": most obvious are jumping to conclusions, impatience, nagging, pressure; less obvious but equally annoying are submitting hastily prepared stories, not proofreading submissions, not taking the time to get the editor's name (or to get it spelled right).

Let's examine some of these faux pas by switching from fortune cookies to a somewhat different publication: *Mad* magazine. I was quite a fan of *Mad* when I was a kid, and something it published way back when sticks with me. In a parody of the film *The Agony and the Ecstasy*, Michelangelo is asked, "When will the painting of the Sistine Chapel be finished?" Michelangelo replies, "When it's finished."

"When will my book be on the press?" the writer asks.

"When it's finished," the editor replies.

I've had people call me three times in a week to see whether I'd completed my end of the project we're working together on. "When will I have an answer?" they ask. I want to say, "When I have one," but I do try to provide a realistic time frame. Don't call anyone three times in one week, unless it's your mother. *She* will love you for it.

It's so easy to become impatient in this business. You are proud of your creative work, and are eager to get it into print and in front of readers. You're eager to see it succeed. Yet, publishing is so often the business of the tortoise. A piece of copy must move through several methodical steps before the ink is laid down on paper. This may seem like plodding to you—sometimes it is just that, but most often it's not.

Three factors conspire to make this a slow-moving business: plain old understaffing, the idea still held by some that there are no mass-production lines in publishing, and the pure mechanics of turning raw words into polished, printed copy. You don't have to like the delays you encounter, but you do have to try to understand why those delays happen in the first place.

HOW LONG SHOULD YOU WAIT?

It doesn't happen often, but it does happen: a writer sends me an unsolicited manuscript and two weeks later writes to ask where his check is. I understand the desire for fast answers to submissions; I myself drop manuscripts into the mail and wish the editor would call me with praise and promises of checks the moment it arrives on his desk. It's a vastly unrealistic wish, and we must work to not get caught up in it.

The fact is that editors are busy people, with many writers demanding their attention. And submissions, frankly, must sometimes take second priority to meeting production deadlines or attending to tens of other details that require concentration *right now*—everything from choosing cover topics to asking writers for revisions, from checking page proofs of something about to go to press to writing the "sell" copy that appears on the magazine's table of contents. If you don't get an answer to a submission right away, hang in a bit.

With magazines, give the editor a month to six weeks to respond to your submission, then write a followup asking if the piece arrived safely. That's a subtle enough hint at this point. If you've heard nothing after another month, drop a note asking when you might have an answer ("Just curious if you've had a chance to look at [name of submission]. Any idea when I can expect to get word on it?"). Then, give it about three weeks. If you still don't have an answer, write a cordial but firm letter requesting one. Don't accuse, don't rant. But do communicate that the time that has passed is excessive. What you do after that is up to you: you can continue to seek an answer, or you can withdraw the submission.

Give book editors and agents more time—they're dealing with much larger packages, after all. The first note should go out after two or three months; the second, after another six weeks; the third, after another six.

Use these timing guidelines for getting answers to unsolicited submissions. You should expect prompter answers to solicited submissions, so trim a week off each of the above intervals when following up on manuscripts you have written on assignment or under contract.

The first two followups should be by mail, unless you have worked with that particular editor three or four times before, and you feel a brief call would be appropriate. You might consider taking to the phone for the third followup (but, as you should with most phone work, follow the call with a recap letter).

Remember the point I made in Chapter 3: to press for an answer increases the chance that that answer will be no.

WAITING OUT THE PRODUCTION PROCESS

Waiting for your manuscript to appear in print can be quite an exercise in patience, too.

Sometimes things can move quickly. When you write for a newspaper, your printed story can appear on doorsteps practically by the time you get home after hand-delivering it to the editor.

Magazines and book publishers can't work as quickly—the "instant books" you've heard about (books that go from manuscript to printed copies in as few as thirty-two hours) notwithstanding.

To show you why, let's look at the schedule of a typical article written for *Writer's Digest*.

You write and mail your query on Jan. 2. It arrives on my desk Jan. 4, but we're in the middle of putting out an issue, so I don't get around to reading it until the 7th. I want second opinions on the query, so I pass it to my other editors. Their responses come back on the 18th. I write you on the 19th, and give you an April 5 deadline.

The story comes in on April 4. Again, it must be reviewed; evaluations return to me on April 18. I write you, asking for revisions by July 1. The revisions arrive on time, we review the piece, and write your letter of acceptance on July 10.

If I were to slot the piece for the next available issue, I have to copy edit and send it to the typesetter no later than July 22. A typeset copy is returned to us by July 28; after proofing it, we send it back to typesetting by our Aug. 1 deadline.

The art department begins work designing the piece and assigning the artwork, and on Aug. 25 we begin compiling all the elements, and starting the physical process called "paste-up" that will lead to the printed copy. Paste-up ends on Sept. 3, when we send the issue to the printer. On Sept. 15, after all final corrections are made, the presses roll. The issue with your article in it—the November issue—appears on the newsstands on Oct. 14.

Note that I said *if* I were to try to get your article into that next available issue. In practice, I can rarely do that, because that space is almost certainly already taken. Space available, then, is one factor determining how quickly your manuscript sees print. Do we have room in the issue for the article? After your article has been typeset and laid out, it might come to four magazine pages, but I have only two pages open. I must select a shorter article. Does that article fit with the other pieces scheduled for that issue, or should we move it back so it can run with some more compatible pieces? For example, an outdoors magazine perhaps wouldn't want to slip your article on camping in the Sierras into an issue that has two other camping articles already scheduled.

Similarly, does the book editor have a slot open in the fall list for your book? Publishers try to release only a certain number of titles at a time. Are other publishers releasing anything similar that time of year? If yes, the publisher might want to push your book back so it doesn't have to compete head-to-head. Would the book sell better on the spring list? Some types of books are seasonal—your book on baseball might sell better in April than in November.

Of course, the more timely the manuscript, the faster we're going to usher it into print. But if your manuscript is of a timeless nature, it could be held for months and sometimes even years before the right spot opens up. Timeless articles are known as "evergreens" in the business. They don't age or wilt or wither. Some articles are bought to serve specifically as evergreens—to be filed and used when a hole opens up.

If your article isn't in print a year after you originally sold it, drop the editor a note asking if he still plans to use it. If yes, hang on.

If no, ask that rights be returned to you, and try to market it elsewhere. Of course, patience here is tested if you don't get paid until the article appears in print—as happens when you sell to a "pay on publication" market. This differs from a "pay on acceptance" market, which sends you your check when it officially accepts the article. But there's little you can do to get the article into print ahead of the editor's schedule. My best advice here is to not sell to pay-on-publication markets. *Never* sell evergreens to them.

Many book contracts stipulate that the manuscript be published by a specific date, and if the book isn't published by then, you have a legal problem, not an etiquette problem. Talk to your lawyer or agent. (And do negotiate to have a clause stipulating a publication date inserted into the contract if it includes no such clause.)

To give you a better idea of the time frame involved in production of a book, let's look at the deadline schedule for *this* book.

I originally discussed the topic with my editor in early January. She asked for a proposal, which I delivered two weeks later. We discussed revisions, and over the next three weeks we revised the proposal twice. It went before the editorial board in mid February.

It was quickly approved, and a contract was drawn up. Deadline for delivery of the book: April 1.

Let me say at this point that discussions of this project moved along at quite a clip for three reasons. 1) My editor and I work in the same office, and didn't have to deal with the delays of sending material back and forth through the mail. 2) This book is short; had I been writing a full-length book, I would have been given a much longer deadline. 3) My editor and I planned the timing of the completion of the proposal to coincide with the meeting of the editorial board, so we got a decision much more quickly than we would have had the proposal been submitted, say, two weeks later, as we would have had to wait for the next board meeting. (Such editorial board meetings happen regularly, but on different schedules at different houses.)

That last point is important. As I mentioned in Chapter 3, decisions on books can take a while because no one person says yes. Groups of people—composed of editors, marketing people, and others—make the decision. The more people involved, the longer it takes to get the decision, and the more patience you have to exhibit.

Back to the production of this book: under ideal circumstances, we would have aimed to deliver the manuscript to the editors a full year before publication date. Twenty-two to thirty weeks would have been allowed for writing the manuscript. (Again, these times vary from publisher to publisher.)

The schedule for producing the book after that April 1 deadline (I must in many cases discuss the projections, not how long it actually took, for obvious reasons) looks like this:

The manuscript is sent out for reading by experts in the publishing field in early April. Most comment is in by early May. Content editing begins on May 15. I receive the content editor's comments on June 2 (quite quick—content editing usually takes a month or more). I deliver the revised draft on June 16 (again, quite quick—it's a short book). The manuscript is sent to the copy editor and to the designer on June 24. I receive a copy-edited version for review on July 1. I must have my copy back by July 10, when the manuscript is delivered to the typesetter via computer disk. I receive printer proofs on July 31; I proofread them and return them on August 7. Corrections are made and proofed, and all corrections are made by August 10. A "dummy" (a layout showing what type will appear on what pages) is prepared using the proofs, and is delivered to the editorial department by August 15. Paste-up begins on August 21, and is completed by August 24, when the book is shipped to the printer. Copies of this book are delivered to the offices of Writer's Digest Books on Oct. 8.

For most books, the writing, selling and production stages will take longer than those described here. Still, no matter what specific times are involved, the process takes longer than what you would expect—and hope for.

A Gentle Nudge

There's not much you can do to combat schedules, but you can spur procrastinating editors along. It's not easy to do, and I can't give you any specific directions for accomplishing it. But I can reveal the secret (it's up to you to put it to use): Enthusiasm and energy are your assets. Use them. Try to instill them into the people you deal with. The best pressure to use on anyone is pressure that they feel internally. Build the pressure within the people you work with. Get them excited about your project. Let them be as eager as you are to see your manuscript in print. Thrill them with the possibility of working with you, a composed professional. *Then* things will move faster. But don't prod and push, don't complain and whine that things are moving too slowly. Yes, the squeaky wheel gets the grease, but the wheel that continues to squeak after it's greased gets replaced.

WHEN IMPATIENCE IS GOOD FOR YOU

There is, of course, a difference between haste and speed. If you do need an answer fast—a go-ahead on a hot article topic, for example—prod until you get what you need. There's courtesy, and then there's your survival as a professional writer.

And I well realize that there are times when exercising patience to infinite limits will gain you nothing. There's patience, and then there's being practical. If you reach the point of being fed up with delays, and believe that production schedules are less at fault than are procrastination and everyday foot-dragging, explain your concerns to the person you're working with (see Chapter 6 for advice on how to do this), and if you aren't satisfied with the explanation you receive (or if you don't get one), see what you can do to back away from the project (more on this in Chapter 11). When patience deteriorates into frustration, it's best to apply your energy to the next project.

In fact, that's good advice to take long before you hit the point of frustration. Never waste time waiting for one particular thing to happen: the editor calling you back, the magazine with your article appearing in your mailbox, the answer to your query finally arriving. Devote yourself to other work. Don't hover around the phone or the mailbox. Watched pots, and all that. . . .

ENTHUSIASM AND EAGERNESS

Try to exercise patience with yourself, as well. Rushing yourself can prove detrimental. Don't rush. Work deliberately, carefully, conscientiously. Meet your deadlines, but no matter how proud you are of your manuscript, no matter how eager you are to get the piece in front of an editor, resist the temptation to yank the last page from the typewriter or printer and slip it into an envelope with one fluid motion. Read it again. Not now. Tomorrow, or in a couple of days. Look at it with a fresh, unloving eye.

Take the time to make certain that your manuscript is accurate. Double-check facts, even if it takes a phone call or two and a couple of extra days. Also ask yourself if the facts that are there are enough. Would the manuscript benefit from your digging up some additional information? Dig it up.

Proofread your manuscript for typographical errors and misspellings, which are downright unprofessional—or *imperfessional*, as one author so imperfessionally spelled it in a letter to me. When editors see misspellings and other such mistakes, they wonder if the writer is ignorant or just plain careless. Then they sit back, realize that it doesn't matter which, and send the manuscript back.

Ask yourself if the writing is as crisp and clear as it can be. If it isn't, revise it until you are happy with it.

Polish it, make it neat, *make it right*. Take the time to do so.

Then put it into the mail.

Remember, *enthusiasm* and *eagerness* are not synonymous. *Eagerness* and *haste* sometimes are. Be enthusiastic, but not hasty.

If you are, you can expect to receive, as my friend at the Chinese restaurant did, good fortune.

"Editor-quette": The Protocol of the Editor-Writer Relationship

The most satisfying type of business relationship I can imagine is represented by the collaboration between writer and editor. We work together to tell stories, to disseminate needed information, to entertain. We take equal and justifiable pride in our contributions to achieving those goals.

In so many senses, editors are your spiritual partners. They're on your side. In book publishing, the editor champions you and your book to other editors, and to the production, art, marketing, and subsidiary rights departments. In magazine publishing, the editor champions the article to other editors and sometimes to the magazine's publisher. In both types of publishing, the editor champions the writing to your audience, giving it a form and a showcase that will appeal to readers and will entice them to buy it.

This noble partnership is made even more satisfying when all dealings are smooth and professional. With that in mind, let's examine an etiquette blueprint for establishing relationships with editors (and, to a lesser extent, with agents).

LAYING THE FOUNDATION

First, enter any dealings with the understanding that editors are, ultimately, customers. No more, and no less. Though they can be friends, they aren't primarily that. Though they can be aides and instructors, they can't be devoted mentors. And though they can be bosses in a loose sense of the word, they are hardly deities demanding genuflection and subservience.

By the same token, a writer is not a creative force endowed with a God-given right to pampering. A writer is a supplier. At its core, the editor-writer relationship is a business relationship.

It's also a relationship between human beings, one that demands not only cooperation but also the respect that makes cooperation possible in the first place. Yes, there are editors and agents who deserve no more respect than do some people who populate the prisons. I can't possibly ask you to respect anyone just because he lists "Editor" as occupation on the 1040 every year. Individual editors are obligated to earn your respect as much as you're obligated to earn theirs.

When I ask you to respect editors, I mean *as a group*. I ask you to respect their roles in midwifing your words into print, as well as their love for and dedication to that midwifery. Most editors don't earn much. Top editors earn top bucks (for that matter, top writers do, too). Yet, for the most part, editors work for love of writing and publishing, not for money.

And, ultimately, respect the *position* editors hold—but not necessarily because they possess, as one of my colleagues phrases it, "the keys to the kingdom." Sure, editors hold a certain power over you, but you must acknowledge more than that power: the fact that these editors *earned* the right to hold the keys. They were hired to perform a job by someone who respected their experience, and who believed in their ability to deliver to readers packages of words that would satisfy them—while making a profit at the same time.

This means not only the top editor, but also everyone you deal with, from assistant editor to copy editor to receptionist. Here's something that's happened to me two or three times, and should never have happened at all: there are a couple of authors I've dealt with directly for a few years—writing them, calling them, editing their manuscripts. When I turned the job of corresponding with these writers over to an assistant, I continued to edit their manuscripts. But an odd thing happened; these authors began complaining to me about how their manuscripts were being copyedited—even though I was still doing that editing. These authors assumed that the assistant was doing the editing, and they suddenly felt free to complain about this person, lesser in their eyes. Consequently, the reputations of these writers were lessened in my eyes.

As a courtesy, as a hallmark of professionalism, as—if nothing else—a survival tactic, demonstrate that you recognize, understand, and believe in editors' rights to do their jobs.

We once worked with a writer who didn't recognize, understand, or believe in that right. He was quick to tell us that he was a professional's professional, but he wrote a letter that was equally quick to tell us otherwise. We had asked this writer to revise a manuscript he had submitted to us on assignment; one request was to rewrite the manuscript's opening paragraphs. "I've read the story, in the form I submitted to you, to my students," he wrote in response, "and everyone was quite taken by it. They listened raptly and said the article was extremely informative and useful. And—without my even asking—two students praised the lead paragraphs. Two of my fellow writing instructors also read it and thought it was well written. I also asked one of my other editors to comment on it and she said she wouldn't change a single word."

I don't care that he disagreed with our rewrite request; I care about the way he disagreed, the way he communicated to me that he valued the opinion of beginning writers above ours, that he showed more respect for their idea of how to run our business than for ours. He was, in essence, calling me and my staff amateurs. I can do without such insults.

Publishing's Processes and Problems

Important to developing that respect is learning what agents do, what editors do, and, in the context of today's publishing world, what writers do—day to day, month to month, year to year. Seeing the publishing process at work will show you how to best deal with your colleagues. More important, though, it will explain their goals and some of the problems they face in trying to achieve those goals. Armed with such understanding, you can become a solution to problems, you'll lessen the risk of becoming a problem yourself, and you'll look considerate and professional in doing so.

I've listed a number of excellent books about writing and publishing beginning on page 123. All will contribute to your understanding of this business, but right now I want to point out two particularly insightful volumes: *Editors on Editing: An Inside View of What Editors Really Do* (revised edition), edited by Gerald Gross, and *A Writer's Guide to Book Publishing* (revised edition), by Richard Balkin.

The books I've listed in the bibliography will also make you comfortable with publishing jargon. We editors have our own lingo (some would call it an argot), and we're reassured, and perhaps even flattered, when you take the pains to learn it. Your commenting that you're willing to submit something on spec, for instance, shows us that you have some background in this field, that you're not a raw beginner. Of course, learning the jargon will also take some of the confusion out of our correspondence—when, for example, I refer to a magazine as a "book," or to a book as a "title." For specifics about publishing terms and jargon, consult *The Writer's Encyclopedia*, edited by Kirk Polking, and the glossary in *Writer's Market*.

BUILDING ON THE FOUNDATION

There are no absolute rules that apply to every contact with every editor and agent, because your working relationship will grow and change as you spend more time on various projects. The editor-writer relationship, just like any other, is dynamic. It lives, and it will change as you and the people you work with get to know each other and become more comfortable with each other. Be prepared to let it grow—and don't force growth upon it.

The best way to build strong relationships with editors is to *listen* to them—out of respect, out of courtesy, but most of all out of necessity. If they ask for manuscripts no longer than 1,500 words, *listen*. Editors mean what they say. They have reasons for the requests they make. Deadlines, manuscript lengths, manuscript focus and slant, information to include in the manuscript—all are specified for a reason. Editors need writing tailored to particular requirements.

And understand that editors are willing to listen to you. Editors always welcome suggestions. They're not, however, so receptive to demands. Suggest an illustration for your magazine article or a graphic concept for your book's cover; don't insist on it. Suggest a title for your book, and fight for it if you believe in it (I do think that you should have quite a bit of say in the final title of your novel), but don't dig in your heels. Suggest ways your book might be marketed, and persist in trying to drum up enthusiasm for the book, but don't complain loudly if the publisher doesn't work quite as hard at marketing as you would like. Again, these are places where it's usually best to defer to the people who make such decisions daily. Remember that the ideal editor-writer relationship is a collaborative one.

Your next step, therefore, is to express, both by attitude and by direct statement, your willingness to work with editors—as peers with a common goal of reader satisfaction, of making a profit, of *excellence*. For example, when you submit a manuscript, say at the end of your cover letter, "If you need more information, please let me know." This demonstrates a considerate attitude toward the editor, and toward the work itself. Tagging the cover letter with "When will this appear?" or "How soon will I be paid?" demonstrates the opposite. It communicates, subtly, that you will drag your heels and perhaps mumble under your breath should the editor feel the manuscript needs extra work. You don't want to sound unconfident ("This article just doesn't seem to flow so I'll understand if you send it back"), but you also don't want to sound too confident that the words you have submitted are perfect and immutable, and too slow to recognize that your colleague, the editor, might be able to improve it by suggesting additional work.

The Closer You Get

Follow the editors' lead in establishing closer working relationships. For example, if they address you by your first name, address them by their first names. I feel a little awkward when I begin a letter of assignment "Dear Jim," and Jim begins his confirmation letter "Dear Mr. Brohaugh." Or if certain editors are consistently slow in returning phone calls, perhaps they simply don't enjoy working on the phone. Write to them instead.

If editors toss a chatty paragraph or two into their letters, respond in kind. Strive for natural, genuine relations with the people you deal with. Here's a sample letter from a writer, written to me: "Enclosed is the article we talked about (OK, I talked, you said, 'Hmmmm,' 'Ohhhh' and 'Wellllll')." Sure, it's silly, but it's not unprofessional—in the context of the relationship the writer and I had already established. When we first began working with each other, the writer tossed a brief, light-hearted remark into his letter. I picked up on it, and tossed something similar back. The comments built on each other. And now, frankly, if this writer ever sent me a completely serious letter, I'd think, "Why is he mad at me?" So, in a sense, he's being more professional by being a little silly, because he's meeting my expectations—but more important, he's being himself.

Just don't get too chummy too fast. One sale to an editor doesn't necessarily lead to a fast and lasting relationship. A track record isn't made by a single winning lap. So often we've bought a manuscript from a writer we've never worked with before, only to have to withstand long, chatty letters from that writer. Some writers drop us notes that say: "Got another article idea. How about something on leads? I'll do it just like the first one." No sale. And some writers commit a more subtle indiscretion: they simply neglect to enclose SASE in submissions following up that first sale.

That's not to say that some writers can't get away with submissions lacking SASE or that the occasional writer doesn't get assignments based only on a topic. One of my writers gets assignments for long profiles and interviews based only on the names he suggests. Two words. But in his case—in the case of every writer who takes liberties with and makes assumptions about our working relationship—as many as a dozen sales to us are already behind him. If he had submitted only a two-word name to us after he had sold his first profile to us, he never would have made it to that twelfth sale. Not even to that second sale.

One thing that dictates, in part, your relationship with an editor is the length and intensity of that relationship *on a single project*. A book writer may deal with a single editor for months, even years. Heavy concentration, by both editor and writer, is given over to that manuscript, from hashing out the outline to developing the manuscript to editing for content to the completion of the final draft. A magazine writer, on the other hand, has much more limited contact with a specific editor. To survive, that magazine writer must be at work on a number of projects for several magazines. The relationship is not nearly as long (though it can grow to be long if you become a regular and trusted contributor), and is hardly as intense as that between book writer and editor. One editor I know likens the difference to that of a marriage and a one-night stand. A crude analogy, perhaps, but apt.

Your relationship with an agent can be defined as a marriage as well—perhaps more appropriately than the relationship with the book editor can. You work with the agent—generally—for a long period of time, on a variety of projects. You share successes and failures, and experience them on a similar level.

The Busyness Factor

Don't let these analogies to spouses and lovers mislead you, though. You cannot reasonably expect the editor you're dealing with to be faithful only to you, to love only your project. To you, your manuscript is your spouse. To your agent or editor, it's an intense fling. You live with it day to day. Your agent and editor meet it often for sweet rendezvous. Book editors can have anywhere from three or four books to a dozen or more going at any one moment. They are acquiring one project, trying to sell the sales staff on another, overseeing the copy editing on a third—all while ushering you through a rewrite. Magazine editors deal with . . . well, I'm not sure you'd believe the number of writers I must pay attention to, so I decided to keep a log of my calls and correspondence for one day. That day was a Monday, which is traditionally a heavy mail day, yet it can be considered representative.

Total pieces of mail addressed to me: thirty-seven (this does not include the forty-one manuscripts, queries and such addressed to other editors). These thirty-seven break down like this: three letters from people who are working with me on assignments (they get immediate answers); one Federal Express package containing slides of upcoming cover artwork from our design director; eleven press releases (none of any interest to me); six complete manuscripts; two batches of poetry; eight queries; one request for information; a manuscript about marriage (and not about writing); a job application; a batch of cartoons; a letter to the editor; and (I'm serious), an eighty-page *something* single-spaced, bound in colored paper, tied together in ribbon, accompanied by a 9"x12" oil painting, and written in French. I *am* serious. And that's the mail alone; I fielded seven phone calls that day.

Agents are just as busy. Mine, as an example, has some seventy other clients. Every one of those seventy expects as much individual attention as I expect. And I'm certain that every one gets as much individual attention as I get.

Now, that's not to say that my agent must deal with every one of the seventy every single day. Nor am I trying to suggest that the number of people any one editor or agent must deal with provides the editor or agent with an excuse to treat any one among the writers poorly or perfunctorily. But you must be aware that other writers and other projects place demands equal to yours; they deserve fair treatment as much as you do.

MAINTENANCE AND UPKEEP OF THE EDITOR-WRITER RELATIONSHIP

Dealing with someone on the long term has its advantages. You get to know your colleague, and you have a good chance to build an enjoyable, productive working relationship. But long-term dealings also present dangers.

For instance, don't expect that the nature of the relationship allows you to take liberties. Yes, there's an intimacy and a comfort that comes with a long-term relationship that would tend to make it easy to take advantage of. For example, as one editor once told me, "Book editors don't like to receive long, chatty letters any more than magazine editors do. It's one thing to keep in touch, another to demand attention."

Also, beware of asking too many favors. Asking for the occasional helping hand presents no problems, but don't become a nuisance. Beware of calling the editor at home, of requesting freebie copies of books or magazines, of asking the editor to use his office photocopy machine to make extra copies of a manuscript for you.

Beware, too, of leaning on editors—that is, depending on them to do *your* job. For example, you can ask editors if they have general information related to your projects on hand, though if such information is available, the editors would likely have offered it to you when the assignment was given in the first place. But ask only if you're working on assignment; it's tacky to request such info if you're working on speculation. You can also ask for specific information, but only if you can find it nowhere else, and if requesting it won't reflect on your credibility as a researcher and writer. Never make a request like this one: "Hi. I'm working on that John Doe profile for you. Would you happen to have Doe's phone number?"

Taking Unfair Advantage

More serious are "favors" that play off your personal relationship with an editor to influence your professional relationship with him. "We've worked together for a long time, and I realize that this isn't my best manuscript, but, hey, we're friends, aren't we?" Not after the editor receives *that* request, you're not.

These problems crop up when writers begin viewing extended dealings with an editor or agent—especially if that person is polite and pleasant and supportive—as the beginnings of a friendship, or even of a relationship on a deeper emotional level. I'm not going to ask that you exclude the possibility of forming true friendships with the people you work with. I include among my professional contacts two or three people who would be my friends even if we didn't share an occupation. I can reasonably expect that they'd put me up in a spare room should I get the opportunity to visit their parts of the country, and they have a standing invitation to use my guest room. But don't misinterpret a kind and supportive relationship with an editor as being a friendship. The ability to work well with an editor doesn't justify your claim to his couch the next time you visit, nor does it warrant any of the other favors and requests and impositions—such as those I discussed above—that a friendship can endure but that anything short of true friendship cannot.

Friendship is *not* an essential component of the publishing process. Samuel S. Vaughan is a long-time editor who spent most of his years with Doubleday. He writes in *Editors on Editing*: "Is the editor required to be your friend? No. Forced friendships work no better in publishing than anywhere else. An editor and an author can work together smoothly if they remain a little distant. A touch of distance may be an asset. Relationships have broken down when an author and an editor become too intimate. When genuine friendship occurs, and it does, of course, it can be wonderful. It had better be genuine; it is certain to be tested."

The long-term relationship can, as I said, lead to even deeper emotions—and deeper trouble. It can lead to emotional dependence. One editor I know tells of working with a writer who asked that he call her every morning and prod her into working on the manuscript that day.

It's not uncommon for writers to call editors to discuss projects, but when those discussions degenerate into confession, lechery, or appeals for psychotherapy, the writers are taking advantage of the working relationship. Editors can be sounding boards, but to use them exclusively for that is to insult them. They cannot serve as psychiatrists. They have no licenses for such work.

As one editor has said, "The advance is the amount of subsidy the writer should expect." Your personal problems are not the problems of your publisher. (That is, unless your personal problems present an obstacle to, for example, meeting deadlines. "If you hit trouble, tell us the instant it happens," says the editor. "Don't wait until after the deadline.")

Dealing with people on the short term—working with magazine editors on the occasional article, for instance—also presents potential for problems, though none quite as serious as those we've just discussed. You must, for instance, be even more wary of taking liberties. While I'll do what I can to grant favors to regular contributors—sending along a copy of one of our books, for instance, or, as happened recently, writing a letter of recommendation to a graduate school our writer was applying to—I can't consider such requests from writers I've worked with only once or twice.

Remember Me?

Perhaps the biggest danger of short-term relationships is that you might slip someone's mind. Therefore, remind the editor who you are when you call or write. Editors can have excellent memories, and editors can have very poor memories. I have been known to write a letter of assignment one week and forget the author's name the next. When the assignment comes in, I'll often see something familiar in the *return address* and put the letter aside for special handling. (That doesn't mean I'm in danger of forgetting the assignment—we have a couple of files that will tell us at a glance everything in progress.) If you are working with an editor for the first time, if you work with that editor infrequently, or if you just haven't corresponded for six months or so, refresh the editor's memory about who you are and what you're up to.

There are three ways you can do this:

1. On the outside envelope, jot—briefly—the nature of the business. "Requested manuscript" or "Requested information" (if it has indeed been requested).

2. Recap previous business early in the letter itself. "Here's my article, 'Effective Memory Jogging,' which you assigned in your letter of 9/23." Or make it friendlier. "Thanks for assigning 'Effective Memory Jogging' to me. I had fun writing it. It's enclosed—about a week in advance of your June 1 deadline." This is especially important if you're submitting something as a result of a phone conversation with the editor. While most editors keep copies of all important mail correspondence, they are somewhat more lax about jotting notes about phone calls. Though I try not to be, I am one of those lax types. I always say to people I've not dealt with before, "Remind me of this phone call in your letter." And I appreciate a quick note that says, "Here's the query for the 'Memory' article we discussed on the phone last Thursday. As you requested, I've enclosed a sample lead and an outline of what I plan to cover. . . ."

3. If you want to, enclose a copy of previous correspondence, though that's hardly essential. As I said, if they're doing their jobs, the editors you deal with will have copies of all important correspondence in their files. That goes for letters making assignments, requesting more information about a manuscript, requesting to see something on spec, and asking for revisions.

Some writers, when submitting a revised article draft, will enclose not only my rewrite letter but also a copy of the original draft. I appreciate the gesture, but it's not necessary with me, as I have copies of both in my files. I'll grant you that other editors might not be so copy-happy, though, and you might be wise to remind them that you have a copy of the original should they need it.

Keep your copy within reach. "One new problem I'm running into," says Greg Daugherty, executive editor of *Sylvia Porter's Personal Finance*, "is writers who never have a copy of their manuscript at hand when the editor calls with questions. The reason, more and more, is that it's in their computer, which doesn't help at that point. I suggest that writers print a second copy for themselves and keep it around until any questions are resolved."

Finally, when it comes to manuscripts and copies and such, there's one "courtesy" that editors can do without. Some writers, when revising a manuscript, "courteously" retype the whole thing (and usually make improvements that the editor didn't request while doing so). The retype has become even more common now that word processors, which eagerly do slave work, like printing out clean copies. This presents two problems: 1) Those improvements I mentioned. Are they really improvements? Or are they alterations that the editor might not like? 2) The editor can't easily see the alterations you made at his request; therefore, he must compare the original copy with the revisions, trying to locate the revised sections so he can check to see if you completed them to his satisfaction. This takes time.

In other words, the "cleanliness" of a freshly typed revision can be misleading—it might still sport problems that the editor can't easily see.

If a rewrite looks like it might be extensive, though, the editor might prefer that you retype it.

Ask the editor if he wants a complete retype when acknowledging his request for revisions. He might ask that you simply type your corrections and additions on separate sheets of paper, and indicate where in the original manuscript they are to be inserted. If you have a word processor and printing a fresh copy is convenient, he might ask that you mark on your fresh copy any material that has been inserted or revised.

Long-term or short, keep the relationship focused. Be considerate of editors' time and workloads by not wasting their time with matters that don't concern them. This advice applies in so many arenas, but the most important among them is in the area of submissions. Do not send material editors could not have the least bit of interest in. Do not send the biking stories to the racquetball magazines or the American fashion retrospective to the science fiction magazine or the batch of three poems to the trade paperback house, or the movie scripts to *Writer's Digest*. This sort of disregard for editors' time, not to mention your own, is as strange as it is inexplicable, as unprofessional as it is maddening.

Even if you have a number of ideas that are perfect for editors, submit one at a time, wait for work on that project to be completed, and *then* propose the next project. Don't inundate editors with material before you've even finished the first assignment. That's not to say that you can't be at work on the next project so you'll have it ready to present at the right time.

Editors prefer to work on only one project with a given writer at one time. More than that, and things can get confusing. As an example in a very physical sense: suppose you send along information to be inserted in the book manuscript you just delivered, and query about another book in the same letter. The editor, seeing the importance of the additional info, routes it to the copy editor for immediate insertion in the book. The letter goes into the file for that book, and the editor never again sees that query.

This advice, of course, doesn't apply to writer-agent dealings. Your agent expects that you will be working on more than one project at a time, so that the agent will be marketing perhaps several of your books at one time.

But when dealing with editors, take the projects one by one. When working on an article, wait until it is written and officially accepted before you propose the next. When working on a book, wait until after the manuscript has been edited and is in production. Don't submit another query shortly after you get an assignment or a contract. Such idea-generation is sometimes viewed as a form of writer's block. Some writers like to have *ideas* accepted, and not necessarily manuscripts. They sell the idea, and never follow through with the story. They sell two, and sometimes three ideas to the same editor, and never deliver manuscript on any of them.

That's more than inconsiderate; that's dangerous. Nothing is more rude, nothing chills a relationship faster, than silence. If you can't finish a story for whatever reason—even if it's a simple matter of changing your mind—let the editor know. He has plans to make, and your story was part of those plans. Have the courtesy to allow him to adjust his plans by knowing that the story he's expecting from you has fallen through.

Less common, and more puzzling, are the writers who invest time and effort in a story, to the point of actually submitting it, and *then* disappear. More than once I've asked a writer to revise an article, only to realize months later that the writer never even bothered to acknowledge my letter. If an editor asks you for revisions you choose not to make, tell him. And explain your reasons. Maybe a compromise can be reached. Maybe it can't—but at least you haven't left someone hanging.

Not long ago, I received a manuscript that we had assigned; I reviewed it, and asked the author for revisions. I waited awhile; the author missed his deadline. Before we could follow up on the revision, the manuscript showed up again in my mailbox. *In an issue of my competitor's magazine!* As I said, if that author had chosen not to make the revisions, I would have been disappointed, but probably not more. If he had withdrawn it and then submitted it to my competitor, I would have had no complaint. As it was, I was infuriated.

KEEP IN TOUCH

Do whatever possible to keep your editor up-to-date and informed about your plans and progress. For example, editors always appreciate:

• Letters acknowledging assignments, and affirming that the deadline and other terms of the assignment are acceptable. (These letters allow you to clear up any questions you might have. If the letter didn't specify pay, the kill fee, the rights he's buying, whether he'd cover expenses, length, deadline, focus of the article, necessity of photos, and so on, you can ask for more information.)

• Acknowledgments of revision requests and a projected date you think you can deliver the revisions.

• Updates on delayed projects or long projects. Such updates are especially important when the project isn't going as smoothly as planned. As I write this, for instance, a freelancer is trying to complete an interview with Stephen King for *Writer's Digest*. This project has been in the works for quite a few months now—King has agreed to the interview, but doesn't have time do it now, with a couple of film projects in the works. Every so often, I'll get a note from the writer: "King's still interested, and we're hoping to set up an interview in a few weeks." A simple update tells me two things: I can expect the interview to land on my desk eventually, and the writer hasn't lost enthusiasm for the project. (When he first encountered scheduling problems, he courteously informed me that he couldn't meet our deadline, and asked if he could get an indefinite extension. I agreed to it.)

Updates are also important on book projects, where you will probably be given a deadline that falls months after you sign the contract. A note saying something like "The first three chapters are completely done, and the next five have been researched on schedule" will gladden a paranoid editor's heart. Also, editors like to know you haven't forgotten such important addenda as the bibliography, the glossary, the illustrations, and so on, and that you plan to send these materials after the manuscript has been completed and mailed. When I submitted the first draft of this book, I included a page that listed what was missing: the acknowledgments, dedication, bibliography, glossary, and index.

• Notifications of when something happens that will affect your story. Suppose, for instance, you were writing a book on how cars are marketed in the United States when Chrysler announced its Saturn line of cars, which would employ revolutionary means—for the car industry, anyway—of pricing and selling cars. Your editor would be pleased and gratified to receive your note saying something to the effect of, "I've noted the introduction of the Saturn line, and will make sure that I cover it in the book. In fact, it looks like it might make an entire chapter all by itself."

Of course, such notifications might have a negative cast, too: "I've tried to get an interview with Lee Iaccoca about Saturn, and he won't give me one until the Saturn cars are on the market, which is after my deadline. Do you have any suggestions?" Either way, it's a matter of keeping everyone informed.

● Notifications of anything that will affect the marketing of the book: a good review, formation of an organization devoted to something related to your book, increased media coverage of the topic of your book that the publisher can use as the basis of new publicity efforts.

Building Good Will

Greg Daugherty of *Sylvia Porter's* points out that writers can show courtesy to editors by proving their value to those editors *indirectly*: "These courtesies don't take a lot of the writer's time and don't cost much money, but can build considerable good will: 1) Referring other good writers to the magazine, and 2) sending clippings and ideas that might interest the magazine, even if the writer doesn't expect to get a story assignment out of it. A writer who shows he's on the lookout for anything useful to the magazine that its staff may have missed can buy a lot of gratitude for the price of a stamp."

CLOSING THE DOOR

There will come a time when you'll find yourself forced to deal with an editor you just don't like. His voice grates, his cigars stink, his letters are haughty, and he never once hints that he has the slightest bit of respect for you and your writing. What should you do?

First, ask yourself if personal clashes are getting in the way of the project you're working on. Answer honestly. Will a grating voice and cigar smoke really affect the quality of your writing? If they won't, get on with the work, and force yourself to be as cordial as possible with the editor.

On the other hand, if his haughty attitude is leading to his giving your manuscript short shrift, if he seems to be discarding your suggestions simply because he doesn't like you or if dealing with him frustrates you so much that you can't stand to look at the manuscript you're preparing for him, point out the problem. Broaching the subject requires calm and diplomacy. Don't accuse; don't fume. Do consult Chapter 11 for some tips on negotiations. Say something to the effect of, "I've been feeling awkward about a couple of matters, and they're starting to distract me from my work." Talk about the problem. Try to solve it.

If you can't, try to get assigned to a new editor.

Write a letter to the editor you've been working with and ask if there isn't another editor inhouse who would be willing to work with you. Explain your request. Be candid but delicate; you don't want to alienate him completely should a switch in editors not be possible. Point out that maintaining the rocky relationship is at the expense of the manuscript.

If that brings no results, consider bringing the problem to the attention of the editor's superior. In the case of a book publisher, you can sometimes check *Literary Market Place* at your library for the name of the editorial director or the editor-in-chief. At a magazine, check the masthead for the editors with those titles.

An attempt to go over your editor's head can backfire on you, however, and cause even more resentment and problems. Better, perhaps, to get on with the work.

If you encounter consistent problems with your agent, on the other hand, sever the relationship as quickly as possible. The agent-writer relationship must be based on mutual respect and trust, or nothing will get done. You must be compatible.

Problems so severe that you would consider resorting to such tactics are, I'm happy to report, relatively rare. And if you maintain a professional, caring attitude when working with editors and agents—if you exercise what one editor has termed "editor-quette"—those problems will become even more rare, and you can concentrate on that pleasant and gratifying collaboration that is at the heart of the editor-writer relationship.

7

Phone Etiquette: In the Manners of Speaking

"I know you're busy," the voice on the phone says to me, "but I hope you don't mind. I'm calling long distance, and I just wanted to—it will take only a few minutes—I just wanted to read you the first few paragraphs of my manuscript. . . ."

I've never hung up on a writer, even though I've received five or six calls similar to that one. The phone is an effective editorial tool, yet there are times when that phone rings that I would like to have been able to have had a talk with that Alexander Graham Bell fellow—by phone or whatever other means were available.

WHEN THE PHONE IS USEFUL

One of the phone's greatest advantages is the speed it lends to business transactions. Use it when immediate response or action is important. For example:

- When your query idea is timely, and you have no time to waste. For example, a celebrity has agreed to an interview with you *tomorrow*, just before he heads out of town.

- When you have a question on an *assignment* (not an on-spec submission) that can be clarified quickly, allowing you to get right to work without waiting for mail to hop cross-country and back.

- When the editor has asked you questions that can be answered quickly and efficiently on the phone.

Another advantage of using the phone lies in the message the medium itself communicates: A call has more immediacy and more impact than a letter, so if you have chosen a call over a letter, the editor feels that you view the matter you're going to discuss as being important—especially if you've corresponded with that editor before. This can backfire, of course, if the call isn't important at all, and the editor feels that it's a waste of time—another reason to use the phone judiciously.

The final advantage is the ability to converse, discuss, and argue. Use the phone when a bit of back-and-forth is required. If the conversation is one-way, however, and especially if that one way is from you to the person you're calling, ask yourself if a letter wouldn't serve just as well.

And, in certain cases, ask yourself if the letter wouldn't serve *even better*. For example, never use the phone to present something that should be presented on paper. A number of writers have called me to say: "Here's my lead sentence. How does it sound?" Well, it might *sound* fine. But how does it read? I won't know until I see it in black and white. On the other hand, the same writers could legitimately have asked, "Does the thrust of the lead seem to fit the article?" That's a question I can answer without seeing something on paper.

Other disadvantages of calling include:

- The phone can be a nuisance. There are days when the phone never stops ringing on an editor's desk. Writers, typesetters, supervisors, marketing people—all are calling with demands and questions and complaints. By the time your call gets through, the editor may have had it.

- A call can waste time. Says Greg Daugherty of *Sylvia Porter's Personal Finance*: "The worst offenders are writers you've never worked with before, or have even heard of, who call up to brainstorm or—still more annoying—to ask what your magazine is all about. I've had writers say to me, 'I was going to send you a query, but thought I'd save time and just call up and bounce a few ideas off you.' Well, maybe that saved the writers' time, but it didn't save mine."

- A call can be *too* immediate. You call with an article idea. The editor might want to think about it, to mull it, as he could if he had a written query in front of him. So, he will do one of two things: he will ask for that written query or he will say no. (Saying no to such requests is so much easier when a quick answer is demanded—and a phone query implicitly makes that demand.)

DISTANCING THE EDITOR

If you do choose to call, don't expect to be treated reverently just because you're calling long distance. Granted, the call is costing you money, and you deserve to have your call handled as expeditiously as possible, but if the person you're calling says, "I'll have to transfer you to someone else" or "Can you hold just a minute?" don't whine, "But I'm calling long distance." After all, *you* chose to call. And besides, if you have to be transferred, you have to be transferred, and noting the length of the connection isn't going to speed things along. As someone once said, some people treat long-distance calls as if they had to walk every mile of the connection themselves.

Time the call to fit not only into your schedule, but also into that of the person you're calling. Business hours are the proverbial 9-5 in most offices. A call anytime during those hours is perfectly acceptable, but some times are better than others. Remember these guidelines:

Calls early in the morning or late in the afternoon risk missing the people you're calling, as do calls around lunchtime. And if you do find the people in at these times, you might catch them settling in for the morning, or getting ready to leave for lunch or for home. In the former instance, they might not be as prepared (or, frankly, as alert) as they'd like to be to deal with you. In the latter, they might be more curt than they would be otherwise so they can keep the call short and stick to their schedules. Also, in my experience, late afternoon is a heavy phone traffic time in general. Best times to call, therefore, would be mid morning, 9:30 to 11, or mid afternoon, 2:30 to 4.

That in mind, don't forget time zones. As a Hawaii-based writer recently reminded me, "Feel free to call with any questions you might have about my submission, but please remember that when it's 10 in the morning for you, it's 5 a.m. for me." You probably won't be calling Hawaii that often, but you will make long-distance calls that cross time lines often enough. If you're in the Eastern time zone, calls to the West Coast before 11 a.m. your time are risky. It's 8 on the Coast; if you're calling an office, no one is likely to be in, and if you're calling someone's house, you're likely to be intruding.

Time-zone problems work both ways. West Coast writers often call me at my Eastern-time-zone office at 9:30 their time. My time, it's half past noon and I'm likely at my favorite Chinese restaurant. Or they'll call at 3:30 their time, 6:30 my time, and I'm on my way home.

The differences in the time zones are more easily forgotten if the Central or Mountain zones are involved; there, the time difference isn't as drastic as it is for an Eastern-Pacific zone call. I have to struggle to remember that when it's 1:30 for me, it's half past noon for my Central time zone writers—and I grew up in the Central time zone.

MAKING CONNECTIONS

When calling, state your name and any previous connection with the editor that might help him remember you. "We worked together on a short piece on phone etiquette about two years back. . . ."

Don't feel impelled to say where you're calling from. This makes me feel as if I've just been put on the clock; I can hear an MCI accountant in the background tallying those seconds. And don't specifically say you're calling long distance—again, the business relationship you are trying to establish has nothing to do with the distance your words must travel.

Keep small talk to a minimum. You want to sound friendly, certainly, but being businesslike is more important right now. Besides, stock small talk can backfire on you. "How are you today?" is a phrase I've heard from every obnoxious phone solicitor who has ever called me.

If you know the call could be an intrusion (but you must make the call anyway), don't aggravate matters by apologizing profusely. Say, "I'm sorry for the intrusion, but this is important," then get down to business. Little is more exasperating than people who waste time apologizing for wasting time. That's a kind of cyclical rudeness.

Down to Business

Next, explain why you're calling in general terms. For example, suppose you and I are working together on a piece, and you have a question about your author's galleys. My managing editor fields the call. You introduce yourself and say, "I'd like to talk to Mr. Brohaugh about my author's galleys."

"Actually, you should be talking to me," the managing editor replies. Or, if someone else fields the call, that person can transfer you to the person you should be talking to.

You can save yourself some of this bouncing around, and save trouble for the people you deal with, by making sure that you ask for the right person in the first place. If you don't know who the right person is, ask the receptionist when you call. "Who handles author's galleys for *Writer's Digest*? Please connect me." This demonstrates that you want to work as efficiently as possible, and that you don't want to force people to waste time transferring calls sent to them because you didn't make your business clear. (This strategy is useful in getting information not only about who to call, but also who to address mail submissions to: "Who is the science fiction editor?" "Who handles questions about late royalty payments?" "Who should I address my query to?") Of course, there's no guarantee that the receptionist knows precisely who you should talk to. You may have to be transferred anyway.

Next, ask the person you're calling if this is a convenient time to talk. Arrange an appointment for your return call if it isn't.

Finally, state your specific business.

Glance at the clock when you first place the call. Try to have the receiver back on the hook within five minutes. That doesn't seem like a very long time—and it isn't, if those five minutes are productively spent. It can seem like a very long time if you spend any significant portion of that time chatting or rambling or wending your way to or away from the point of the call. Also, when you next receive a phone bill that includes business calls, look at more than just what those calls cost you. See how long you kept the other parties on the line.

I don't mean to tell you that all calls should be cut short after five minutes. If the call takes a half hour because it must take that long for both of you to conclude your business, let it go that long. Or longer.

Graceful Goodbyes

When it's time to end the call, end it quickly. Don't be abrupt, but don't let the call wander off aimlessly into the afternoon, either.

Pay particular attention to human "busy signals"—hints from those you're calling that they're busy and that it's time to sign off. One of my signals is summing up the call: "OK, then, I'll look forward to seeing the manuscript next week." And when I get to "Thanks for calling," you know the receiver is halfway between my ear and the hook.

If someone comes straight out and says he must go, let him go. Don't impose by continuing the conversation. I once told a caller: "Can we talk tomorrow? I have to pick up my child in a half hour, so I really must go." He said, "Then I'll keep it short." When I told him—twice—in the next ten minutes that "I really do have to go," I nearly reached that point of hanging up on someone.

The ideal, of course, is to not let the conversation go on so long that the person you're talking to must drop hints. *You* called; *you* bring the call to an efficient and graceful close.

If the person you're calling isn't in, leave a complete message with whomever or whatever answers, human being or machine:

● *Your name.* Spell it. Often, even if you have a simple name, the person on the other end of the line might not hear exactly what you say, and will guess at a spelling. The person you're calling may be expecting you to call, but if the message you leave doesn't make it clear that you indeed were the person who called, you might not get a return call.

Don't leave just your first name, even if you know the person you're calling very well. If you say to that person, "Hi, this is Fred," he'll probably know who you are—because he recognizes your voice in addition to your name. If, however, someone else takes a message that says simply, "Call Fred," he might wonder, "Which one? The writer? My son? The editor down the hall?"

● *A brief statement of the nature of your business.* Again, if the person you're calling doesn't recognize your name and doesn't have any idea of what you want, she just might not return the call. If she does, you have just imposed on her to invest time in a call that perhaps she doesn't have to make. Suppose, again, that you're calling me about author's galleys. I'm not in, so the receptionist takes a message; you don't mention the specifics of the problem, though. When I call back to find out what you wanted, I'll discover—too late—that our managing editor, who handles galleys, should have been the one to make the call.

Also, if you state your business, the person taking the call might be able to help. Our managing editor takes his share of calls for me when I'm away from my desk; as I noted before, you could have cleared up the galley problem immediately had you stated your business clearly.

● *The urgency of your business.* If the person you're trying to reach must get back to you immediately, say so. If the return call can wait until tomorrow, say that.

● *Your phone number.* Leave the number even if you know that the person you're calling has it on file. This saves the trouble of digging it out. If you have an extension number, leave that, too; it removes an additional barrier in getting back to you.

● *A time to reach you*, especially if you're not going to be available for a stretch of time longer than a half hour to an hour.

Do this each time you call, but remember that you can be too explicit when leaving messages. Whenever I'd reach the answering machine of one of our regular contributors, I'd leave this message: "Hi, John. This is Bill Brohaugh of *Writer's Digest* calling. . . ." After some *years* (yes, years) of this, John asked me, "Why do you always say you're with *WD* when you leave a message? How many Bill Brohaughs do I know? Besides, after all this time, if you grunted into the recorder, I'd know it was you calling because I can recognize your voice."

DON'T PHONE HOME

Like most of society, editors and agents work at work, and enjoy personal lives at home. There are three times when you can call editors at home:

1. When they invite you to. Many editors work at home where interruptions have more difficulty finding them, and part of that work might be on your manuscript. If they want to hear from you during that work time—which, for many editors, extends into the late evening—they will tell you so.

2. When you have a *serious* problem that must be dealt with immediately. I've been lucky this way; I've received only one such call, from one of my regular writers telling me that a manuscript I was expecting the next day—and needed that day—had been delayed for whatever reason. We had to figure out how to solve the problem.

The call was important—I had to have the information first thing in the morning (which would have been 5 in the morning for that writer, who lives on the West Coast—thus his choice to call me at home), and the writer kept the call brief. Therefore, I wasn't annoyed by the interruption; I appreciated it.

Perhaps I'm a bit accepting in this regard. Evan Marshall, of the Sterling Lord Agency, represents another opinion: "To me, and to most people I know, calling an editor/agent at home is the ultimate no-no. Even if a writer has a serious problem that must be dealt with immediately, it should still be absolutely *verboten* for him to call the editor at home without the editor having given him permission beforehand. In my experience, a writer with an emergency calls the editor's office, tells the editor's assistant or secretary that he must speak to the editor on urgent business, and then it's up to the discretion of the assistant to either give out her boss's number, or to say she'll call her boss and either have him call the writer or call back herself with instructions. If the problem arises outside of business hours, I think it should still wait. How many problems really can't?" Marshall has a good point: problems that must be dealt with *immediately*, that can't wait until the next business day, are quite rare. The exception here is if you won't be available the next business day—if you're about to go on a trip, for instance, and something must be cleared up before you leave.

3. When your hours dictate your calling after hours. For example, one agent tells of a client who works as an attorney; he is in court all day and can't call during normal business hours. Even if this type of situation applies to you, though, weigh the necessity of calling. Would a letter do just as well?

Agents are particularly susceptible to the call at home, because of the more intimate nature of their relationship with writers, who tend to perceive their agents as being more business partner—indeed, more friend—than they do the average editor. Writers might call editors to ask questions about how a manuscript should be written, or what to do now that an important source has backed out of an interview, or some other facet of a specific project. Those same writers might call their agents for the same reasons, but they might also call to *chat*, to receive reassurances, to dispel some loneliness, to reach out, as Ma Bell has been asking us to do for years. The agents might be perfectly willing to chat, reassure, dispel, or otherwise be reached, but they're more likely to want to do that during business hours—unless, again, they specifically invite calls at home. (Also, this doesn't mean you should indulge in chatting, etc. Note that I said that agents *might* be willing. It all depends on the nature of your relationship.)

The disadvantages of calling editors and agents at home include:

1. If you're calling about business—royalty statements or the finer points of a manuscript's editing—the person you're calling has almost certainly left the relevant documents—the statements or the manuscript or whatever—at the office.

2. You might interrupt: meals, chores, a family argument, visitors, sleep, or (as is likely in my case) a rousing game of pinball.

3. You might find the person you're calling in an "at-home" frame of mind, which might be testier, less patient, more lackadaisical, or more apathetic than his "in-office" (that is, professional) frame of mind.

If you *must* call people at home, *never* call after 9 in the evening, their time.

FINAL WORDS

I'll leave you with these additional telephone guidelines before I ring off:

• Don't call the editorial office three days after you dropped the manuscript in the mail—especially if the manuscript wasn't solicited. The editor almost certainly doesn't have an answer for you yet. And even if she does, she may prefer to give you that answer via the mail. If you make a followup call this quickly, you are abusing the immediacy of the phone call in an exhibition of haste.

• Don't call collect—unless you're invited to. It's presumptuous. And as annoying to publishers as the collect call is the abuse of the toll-free 800 number. Some publishers provide toll-free 800 numbers for the convenience of customers placing orders. You are not a customer placing an order. Don't tie up the lines. Again, you are taking advantage with no permission to do so.

• Similarly, don't call on your nickel to ask minor questions or just to chat, and then later bill the magazine for these "expenses." The cost of calls for research can be expensed legitimately, but it's not wise to ask to be reimbursed for calls to the magazine or book editor, unless the editor has approved such billing.

- There is something similar to the SASE for phone calls: offering to accept a collect call from an editor. I've seen this offer made at the end of query letters, and I view it as gracious, although some editors think this sounds too eager and subservient. I've never taken a writer up on the offer. If I want to make the call, I should spring for it.

- If you want to discuss your manuscript—revisions the editor has requested, for instance—call the editor in advance, set up an appointment to call later, and explain what you want to discuss. This will allow the editor time to pull a copy of the manuscript and any related correspondence from the files so he'll have it in front of him when you talk.

- Take notes about phone calls, and file them. If you think the person you talked with should have a record of the call in her files as well, follow the call with a letter recapping the call. "This is just to confirm our conversation of 3/15, in which you gave me the go-ahead to write. . . ." Remember, though, that if the confirmation letter accomplishes exactly what the call did, you probably could have skipped the call.

- Remember that the phone gives you a certain power over the person you're calling. Ever notice how people give priority to a ringing phone? In stores, for instance, clerks will abandon you while they dash away to pick up the phone. If you need immediate attention from an editor or agent, call. Remember the power of the phone. But remember also its power to annoy.

In-Person Etiquette

I suppose it seems odd that a book of etiquette doesn't discuss face-to-face relationships until the eighth chapter, since so many principles of general etiquette are based on concerns related to meeting people, talking with them, dealing with them in person.

Consider, though, that publishing business is usually conducted through the mail and over the phone. I've dealt with some writers for ten years without ever meeting them in person. The whole of our relationship exists on paper or in electronic signals over phone lines.

Still, you'll find frequent opportunities to meet with editors and agents in their offices, over lunch, at writers conferences. Also, a face-to-face meeting with an information source is more than just likely; it's often essential to the story you're writing. The quality of personality profiles, for instance, depends in part on the writers' physical descriptions of the subjects and their surroundings. To make readers feel that they are "there," the writers must have gotten there themselves.

OVER-THE-THRESHOLD SUBMISSIONS

There are three reasons to visit the office of an editor or agent: to pitch ideas or new projects, to discuss a project that is already underway, and to say hello.

Each of these cases requires that you have had some previous dealings with the editor or agent. Few editors are willing to spend time listening to proposals for books or articles from writers they've never dealt with before. Even fewer will talk with writers who just want to stop by and see the offices and meet with an editor they'd like to sell to someday.

On the other hand, those same editors will be eager to chat with writers whose work they've purchased, writers whose phone voices are the only thing they could recognize. There are many writers I've worked with who I'd be pleased to have stop by my office in Cincinnati. Depending on how long we've worked together, I'd probably extend them a dinner invitation, or an offer to go to a ball game. Just so we can get acquainted.

A business tip, though: Never make a purely social call. Be prepared to discuss some business. First, you never want to squander an opportunity, and second, you want to be able to claim the trip as business expense to the IRS legitimately.

Visiting so you can discuss projects already underway—say, the revision of a book chapter—of course demands an already-established working relationship. Usually the editor, not you, will suggest such a working meeting. If you feel such a meeting would be helpful, recommend it. But such meetings are necessary only when the work to be done is extensive, and when sitting together at a table with the manuscript in front of you will facilitate the discussion. Most article rewrites, for instance, can be worked out through the mail or with a couple of phone calls.

If you want to meet with your editor or agent:

- Set up an appointment, and make it specific ("2:30 Thursday," not, "Is it OK if I drop by sometime before the end of next week?").

- Explain the nature of the proposed meeting, so the editor can decide if the meeting will be worthwhile, and can have any needed files or copies of manuscripts or whatever on hand when you arrive.

- Estimate how long it will take, so the editor can maintain control over her schedule.

These guidelines also apply to setting up meetings with interview subjects. (See Chapter 9 for more on setting up and conducting interviews.)

Once in the editor's office, conduct your business efficiently, and stick to the time estimate you gave when setting up your appointment. But don't feel that you can't chat a bit. Small talk and friendly exchanges are an expected part of conversation, after all, and this meeting you've arranged can certainly be considered a conversation as well as a sales pitch.

Don't expect that the personal contact will automatically sell your ideas. A personal visit is simply a sales tool, not a guarantee.

Do expect the editor to ask you to outline your ideas further on paper later. The writing sells, and the editor must see a sample. Some editors—depending on how well they know you—will give you an assignment on the spot, but will usually ask for elaboration before you actually begin writing the assignment. Others will simply indicate if they are interested, and ask that you put your proposal on paper.

BUSINESS LUNCHES AND ENTERTAINMENT

You'll sometime have the opportunity to meet an editor or agent over lunch or drinks for one or more of the reasons you'd meet him at the office: to discuss projects or just to get acquainted. The setting is a bit different; so is the etiquette, though there are far more similarities than there are differences.

There has arisen a whole school of "power lunching"—"digest for success," I suppose you might call it—that details the implicit "language" of what you order and how you order it and other such pickable nits. If you subscribe to such theories, fine. Follow them. But I prefer friendly lunching: enjoy the meal, and use it as a foundation for a relaxed and productive business meeting.

One of the biggest issues involved in lunchtime etiquette concerns this question: *Who reaches for the check?*

The answer lies in this question: *Who invited whom?* The person who extended the invitation usually has the most to gain from the meeting, and should pay for the lunch or whatever. An exception to this is if you're lunching with an information source: even if the *source* recommends that you talk over a meal or drinks, *you* pay the tab. Don't invite accusations of having been *bought* by the source—a couple of drinks or even a nice meal may not seem like much of a price for buying someone, but it can be construed as a payment nonetheless.

Occasionally people on expense accounts have latitude in what they can pay for—which sometimes makes them more willing to reach for the check first, even if you theoretically should pay. If you have arranged a meeting with, for instance, an editor about a legitimate business concern—revisions, for example—it's not out of the question for the editor to pay. That's because, in almost every case, the editor will expense the lunch to his company. But never invite yourself to lunch, thinking that the editor will automatically pay, or that it's the publisher's function to lunch writers. "In my days as a book editor," says agent Evan Marshall, "there were several writers I knew reasonably well who would call me periodically and hint around about lunch until I issued an invitation. At the lunch, these writers would proceed to order as if they hadn't eaten for days. Two or three cocktails, the most expensive appetizer and entree, a glass of wine with the meal, the biggest dessert, more to drink. One writer even ordered a second dessert, after I had settled up the tab. These types make editors feel used. They also make editors feel that the writers are pretty hard up—i.e., they're not doing very well— i.e., they couldn't be very good. It's a pathetic sight."

If you have instigated the lunch, reach for the check. If the other party allows you to take it, that's the end of the discussion. If he says something to the effect of, "Why don't you let me take care of it?", protest politely. If the other party insists, go along with it. Whatever you do, don't get into a squabble about the check. It's not that big a deal. But if the other party is an information source, be firm.

There isn't much "dutch" dining in the world of publishing. Only when dining with someone who is as much friend as business associate should you comfortably start tallying up who ordered the soup and who had two iced teas—and only then if the meeting was on a *purely* social basis. The editors of a then-new regional magazine once asked a colleague of mine to lunch, whereupon they grilled him for advice about their magazine and the direction they should take. When lunch was over, the editors reached for the check. Then they reached for a calculator to figure out my friend's share of the bill. That's not just rude and tacky, that's infuriating. And my friend was indeed infuriated.

If you're meeting with someone for drinks, the "dutch" arrangement of paying for alternate rounds is acceptable. But remember, in drink as in food, offering to pay demonstrates respect for your companion, as well as gratitude for her time and help. (Remember that you can deduct the cost of such entertainment from your taxes—consult IRS publication #463.)

I see no need to alter the above guidelines for different gender situations—a fancy phrase for "if the host is a boy and the guest a girl or vice versa or if they're both the same sex." Business is business, no matter what sex you and your colleague are.

If you're dining as a guest of someone else, don't take advantage. Don't order steak if your host is ordering the chicken salad. Follow your host's lead. But don't be a slave to it. If your host orders steak, and you *like* chicken salad, by all means order it.

WRITERS CONFERENCES

Attending a writers conference offers you a wonderful chance to meet and chat with editors, agents, and fellow writers—and to conduct some business, if the opportunity presents itself. Most of the meeting and chatting is done informally, after lecture sessions and at parties and other social gatherings. Some conferences set up writer-editor meetings on a more formal basis: you set up an appointment with one of the conference speakers who answers your questions, or, more likely, critiques a manuscript you submitted in advance of the conference.

If you get a chance to talk to speakers informally, don't monopolize them—out of courtesy not only to the speaker, but also to the other writers attending the conference. Feel free to track speakers down between sessions; just be careful to not delay them from their next obligations. They may be on their way to give another lecture, or to sit on a panel, or to attend one of the other sessions: the speakers are there to learn, too. Says agent Evan Marshall: "At one conference, the only way I could get away from a particularly persistent female writer was to duck into a nearby men's room—and even then I wasn't sure she wouldn't follow me in, manuscript in hand." And when talking with a speaker, allow other people to ask their questions. If you'd like to offer to buy a speaker a drink or a snack, do so—but welcome other people to join you.

In fact, you should never be afraid to join such informal conferences. If you spot a speaker chatting with other conference attendees or even with other speakers over coffee or in the hall between sessions, don't feel that you're intruding if you walk up to them, introduce yourself, explain that you're attending the conference (though that will probably be evident by the name tag you'll likely be wearing), and ask if you may join in.

Limit such confabs to "conference territory": the physical grounds of the conference and its immediate environs. Should you run into speakers at area restaurants, or as they're sightseeing or sunning themselves or doing whatever else they might be doing in their free time, respect the fact that they're "off the clock." You don't have to avoid them or hide. Smile, say hello, bandy small talk. But don't start cross-examining them.

And please, never bother conference speakers in their hotel or motel rooms. Don't call; don't drop by.

Selling On-Site

Most important, look at a writers conference as an *opportunity* to conduct business—not as an *invitation* to do so. The speakers might be willing to talk about ideas for their magazines or publishers or agencies. And they might not. Inquire politely.

Limit the business to pitching general ideas to editors or agents. Don't submit actual manuscript copy; they are ill-equipped to carry submissions back home with them, and they're certainly not going to buy any manuscripts on the spot.

Nor are they going to commit to any ideas then and there. If you pitch ideas, the response you get will be either "Sounds interesting; send me a query," or "Sorry." If an editor *is* interested, follow up through normal submission channels—through the mail.

A while back I spoke at a conference in Northern Wisconsin. At lunch the day of my speech, some of the people attending the conference joined my table.

"What's the easiest way for a writer to break into *Writer's Digest*?" one of them, a woman named C.J. Fosdick, asked late in our conversation.

"It's a tough sell," I said, "but writers new to us most often break in with a Chronicle or a Writing Life item."

She asked about what sort of Chronicles I was seeking, and when I told her, she asked, "Would you mind if I submitted something to you?"

"No guarantees—but I'll take a look."

I liked what I saw when the article came in—and I liked the way

Fosdick had conducted herself before submitting the piece. She did not, you'll notice, shove a manuscript at me over the salad. She alerted me to the manuscript, allowed me to learn something about her so that I would connect a person with the submission when I received it, then submitted the piece to me at my office after she returned home.

We printed the article just a few months later.

Many writers have found their agents in much the same way. Jean Auel met the woman who would eventually become her agent, and who would sell Auel's *The Clan of the Cave Bear*, at a writers conference.

DRESS FOR RESPECT

Meeting people in person places certain demands on your demeanor and dress. For the most part, those demands differ little from those of any face-to-face meeting, but your standing as a writer places a few extra requirements on you.

In your home office, no one cares how many holes there are in your jeans (mine, as I type this, have three holes and two worn spots that will mature into holes by the time I finish this parenthetical thought). We like that freedom. The writing lifestyle allows us to choose to be casual. But when we sit down to lunch with an interview subject or with an editor, some of that choice is removed.

My primary rule about clothing is this: *Dress to demonstrate respect*. Respect, remember, is not a matter of admiration, though admiration does enter into it. Respect involves understanding and compassion. Communicate these in your dress.

When you visit an editor's office to pitch ideas, dress as if you were going on a job interview, which, in sense, you are.

When meeting with interview sources, though, the guidelines aren't quite as clearcut. There are many times when you'd dress as you would in a job interview, particularly if the source is a company president, a civil authority, or a person in some other position of power.

But suppose you wanted to interview my father. I'd recommend that you leave the suit or the dress at home. My father is an automobile mechanic (a fine one, I might add, so I can see why someone might want to interview him to tap his expertise). If you were to visit his garage wearing a three-piece suit, he might think you a bit uppity, a bit condescending. He will think you a little strange at the least, and an outsider at the worst. An outsider he might not feel comfortable talking to. Dress near the level of the person you're meeting to demonstrate the *understanding* I mentioned before. You'd be better off wearing a pair of slacks and a dress shirt. And even that might not be necessary or—considering the grease you're likely to encounter—practical. There are times when you must choose comfort and practicality over spiffiness: if, for example, you were interviewing the director of a museum who will give you a tour. You're crazy if you don't wear comfortable shoes.

A more severe example of the need to dress for respect is Diane Sawyer's visit to Iran for an episode of *60 Minutes*. The Iranians allowed her and her camera crew to visit Tehran if she met certain conditions, one of which was to wear something on her head whenever she was in public. She complied. She may have looked oddly 1950ish to the '80s Americans watching her reports, but she couldn't have gotten her story without dressing in a way that showed respect not just to Iranian custom, but also to the Iranians themselves.

The same guidelines apply for conferring with editors, though you can afford to be a little more casual on such occasions. Despite all you've heard about corporate takeovers of book publishers and their increased concern with that business preoccupation, the bottom line, the inside of an editorial office in no way resembles the halls of IBM's corporate headquarters. Sure, you'll see your share of suits and ties and fashionable dresses. But you'll also see your share of open collars, sweaters, sports shirts, and, depending on the whims of fashion, slacks. This means that you don't have to drag out your three-piece when visiting those offices. A suit or dress is acceptable, as is a clean pair of slacks and a dress shirt or blouse. There's not much way you can vastly underdress the editor you're meeting with, and editors—whose creativity and attitudes toward dress aren't terribly different from yours—more or less expect these creative artists called writers to be somewhat free-wheeling and individual.

But there are limits. Be neat. Be clean. Be respectful. Be patchless. And, yes, be comfortable. And be aware of the signals that your dress communicates not only about *you*, but also about *your writing*—especially about the writing you will do for that editor. For example, do you think John Molloy wore tennis sweats when meeting with the editor of his *Dress for Success*? If you were an editor, would you trust someone wearing a Nehru jacket while proposing to write about trends developing in American society?

Writers conference dress is easily classifiable. If you're speaking at the conference, dress up.

If you're attending the conference, wear comfortable clothes. You'll be running around a lot, from session to lunch to sales room to session to coffee pot. You'll be doing a lot of chatting. At chats, you dress comfortably. You dress formally at debates and at the UN. Should you arrange a brief meeting with an editor to talk story ideas, slip on a tie—if you want to. That editor, understanding the points I've just made, expects you to dress casually.

Consider dressing up for anything labeled a banquet if it meets one or more of these conditions:

1. It is the final event of the conference.

2. It is held in the evening.

3. Awards will be presented (especially if you might receive one).

4. There is sufficient time to get dressed. (Some banquets are held shortly after the final session of the conference. In such cases, I see no point in dashing to your room—particularly if you're lodging more than a couple of blocks away—to dress. Nor do I see any point in dressing up for an entire day's worth of sessions because you're anticipating the banquet.)

THE PROTOCOL OF PERSONAL HABITS

Gum is out in almost every situation. If you're at a writers conference and part of the audience at a lecture, or by yourself, OK, indulge yourself. But, please, never when talking to anyone.

If you visit someone's office or home to conduct an interview, I advise against asking for coffee. Accept it if it's offered (and, of course, if you want it.)

Cigarettes are chancy at best. Follow the lead of the person you're talking to. If she lights up, you can feel comfortable doing the same. But don't let the cigarette get in the way of what you're doing. Puffing and taking notes simultaneously is difficult.

One situation where it's permissible to ask the person you're visiting for coffee, or if you can smoke even if the other is a nonsmoker, is when you are sitting down to what is likely to be a long work session—say, a meeting with an editor to discuss lengthy revisions for the book you're writing. Ask for coffee; ask where the sandwich machines are. Ask if your colleague minds your smoking. (My general advice is to forego the cigarettes entirely, but remember that I am a nonsmoker.)

Drinking is another matter entirely. Remember these guidelines:

- As with cigarettes, follow the other person's lead. If you're lunching and he orders a beer, feel free to order a drink for yourself. Best to keep it to one, or, at most, two, at business lunches, though.

- If you don't drink, feel *no* pressure to do so. If the other orders a drink, you will insult no one if you opt for coffee.

- At any sort of party—a publication party, or a "happy hour" at a conference—don't feel tied to that one or two limit. But keep it in moderation. Don't embarrass yourself, and don't let drinking get in the way of any business that might be conducted. Don't risk meeting potentially important contacts only to later forget their names. Or suppose an agent shows interest in your work; keep yourself in condition to discuss it as articulately as possible. But there's a more important courtesy at work in this matter of drinking: courtesy to yourself. Respect yourself, and make sure you can drive home safely.

And drugs? Need we even discuss them? If you get into a situation where sources or editors offer some recreational drugs, you've entered a league far different from mine. It's my opinion—and you can think it puritanical, I don't care—that drugs can destroy more than relationships. They can destroy you. They can destroy your talent, your skills. Again, respect yourself; avoid them. And should you encounter them in a publishing social circle or even in a business situation, decline.

FINAL WORDS

I suppose I should mention that most general rules of etiquette apply when meeting people—you know, wear shoes in editor's offices and don't spit during lunch and that sort of thing—but I suppose you've already thought of these. . . .

Sources of Respect/
Respect of Sources

The people you interview or who otherwise supply you information for your writing require (and deserve) special courtesy. They are co-operating with you often for no reason other than that they're nice folks. Yes, some people are used to dealing with curious people, if not media people specifically: public officials, public relations people at companies and organizations, researchers, doctors, and lawyers, librarians, and teachers, especially on the college level. Most, however, are not: the accountant you question for tips for your article on filing taxes, the octogenarian you chat with for reminiscences for your historical novel, the shop owner you profile for the feature section of your local newspaper.

For the most part, the advice I give here applies to dealing with that latter group, those everyday people who are more or less willing to cooperate with you—and in fact might be excited about having the spotlight sweep across them for just a moment (they might be afraid of that, too—keep that in mind). They have something to share, nothing to hide.

My advice has limited application if you're writing exposés or investigative reports. Investigative journalism has an etiquette all its own, but that etiquette is closely tied into matters of ethics, and this book doesn't aspire to deal with ethics in any detail.

Also, keep in mind that this is not a short course in interviewing and information-gathering technique. I'm describing here only the courtesies you should extend to your sources. For more on how to dig out the information and quotes you seek, consult John Brady's *The Craft of Interviewing* (Vintage).

Many of the courtesies I've described elsewhere in this book apply: the phone manners and mail etiquette and person-to-person courtesies I've previously discussed apply to sources as well as to editors and agents. For example, a major part of the etiquette of dealing with sources lies in your general dress and demeanor. To refresh your memory, refer back to Chapter 8.

BEFORE THE INTERVIEW

Whether you're planning to interview someone over the phone or to meet your source in person, call in advance—when possible—to set up an interview.

Make the initial call to set up interviews to the subjects' work phone. There they are in the "conducting business" mode; you'll catch them off guard if you call them at home.

Introduce yourself, and explain why you're calling. Explain the purpose of your proposed interview, and the topics likely to be covered. (This will allow the subjects some time to collect their thoughts before they sit down to talk with you.) Also describe in general terms who you are, and who you represent. If you don't have an assignment—only an idea that an article would probably sell—say, "I'm working on an article that I'd like to eventually show to the sports magazines," or whatever.

If you do have an assignment, use it as a lever. "The city magazine here in town has asked me to write an article for them, and. . . ." If the magazine has agreed to look at your article on speculation but hasn't given you an assignment, say "The city magazine has expressed an interest in my article." Remember that some people, particularly celebrities, won't talk to writers who aren't working on assignment—which is their choice. It is a courtesy to explain, when setting up the interview, whether you do or don't have a commitment from an editor. But if you don't have that commitment, you could lose the opportunity to get the interview. Try this: if you have an assignment (or if the editor has said he will give you one if the source agrees to talk to you), say so. If you have no assignment, don't broadcast that fact. If, however, the source asks if you have an assignment, answer honestly. Whatever you do, don't try to get an interview by saying you're representing such and such a magazine, when that magazine hasn't given you a specific assignment. That's gauche, not to mention unethical. You can, as I said, say that the magazine has expressed interest (if it has), but you can't imply that the magazine has given you any guarantee that the piece will appear in print.

The everyday person who hasn't had much contact with the press probably won't care if you're working on spec or not.

The Well-Appointed Interview

If your potential interviewee agrees to the interview, set up an appointment. Give a specific and realistic estimate of the interview's length. Then ask for a convenient time and place to talk. When I say *place*, I'm referring to both phone and in-person interviews: some people would rather not be interviewed while they're on the job; the interview is stealing productive time, and the subjects' employers might frown on that. One of the agents I interviewed for this book requested that we speak during the evening, when she was at home, because of her busy work schedule. Therefore, if they'd rather you call them at home or meet them at lunch when they're more relaxed and, in some situations, can be more open, you give them the opportunity to say so by setting up an appointment.

My advice for setting up a time for the interview takes for granted that the subject is willing to be interviewed. If you want to talk to someone about a sensitive subject, it wouldn't be wise to allow the subject to stew about it. Pose your questions then and there.

Sometimes when you ask to set up the interview, the subject will say, "Right now would be fine." In that case, make sure that "right now" is fine for you, too; have your questions, your tape recorder and your pen ready—unless, of course, you were calling to set up an in-person interview. You won't want to go along with speaking to the source then and there. After all, you have a good reason for wanting to meet the source in person, don't you? Explain that reason to the source when setting up the interview—that you'd like to meet in the subject's office so you can write about her working environment, or that you'd like to take photos of the subject. But if you have no reason for meeting the source, why not simply conduct the interview over the phone?

If you're under time pressure, tell the subject exactly how much time you have. If a deadline faces you, you could, for instance, call in the morning to set up a phone interview for that afternoon. Try to set interviews a few days or a few weeks in advance, though, so the source can easily fit it into his schedule.

THE INTERVIEW ITSELF

Come to the in-person interview prepared with notebook, pens and pencils, and working tape recorder. Asking to borrow a pen is more than rude and embarrassing; it casts doubt on your credibility and professionalism.

Take your pictures before or after the interview or both, not during, even if another photographer and not you is taking them. Photography during the interview will unnerve the subject, or just plain distract her.

Unless your sources are in that category of people who deal frequently with reporters and writers, they have no true understanding of the publication business. For instance, it's likely that they won't understand why you don't write down and print everything they say. Therefore, at the beginning of any interview, explain as much as possible about what you're doing and why—to interest your sources, and to keep them from expecting too much from the eventual printed material.

Also, explaining the purpose of the material you're writing will help them tailor their comments to your needs. But if that particular courtesy will get in the way of your getting the information—if complete honesty will make a source back away ("I'm doing a story on supposed ineptitudes in city council. . . ."), you don't necessarily have to extend the courtesy. The source will likely ask anyway, though, so have your answer prepared. One answer—and usually it's an answer that reflects the absolute truth—is that you don't know how the information will be used. "I'm just beginning to investigate this. I know my topic, but I won't be shaping the story itself until I've done all my research." You can use that answer with absolute integrity, because, after all, you shouldn't shape your story until you have all your information.

Also explain how extensively sources' contributions will be used. If their quotes will be used only to supplement information from other sources, tell them, so that they won't expect to find a profile of only themselves. If they will not be quoted at all—if you're seeking background information only—let them know that.

If you're unsure about either point, be upfront and say so—once again, you won't know how the story will turn out until you begin writing it.

When you explain when and where the material is likely to appear, give an honest appraisal of the article's chances of actually seeing print. If you're writing a piece on speculation with no guarantee that it will be published, say so. This will prevent your sources from waiting endlessly for a story to appear should it fall through, and will delight them should the article, which they were seeing as tentative, finally appear.

At Ease

Remember that the everyday person might be intimidated by the concept of the interview. So be as relaxed as you can, and conduct your interview as if it were simply a conversation with someone you find interesting.

Listen to your subject—too few of the writers I have dealt with do that. Listen out of courtesy, and listen for intriguing statements that can be expanded, and forget your prepared questions for a few minutes while you go after this new information. The only difference between interviewing and real conversation is that *you* don't offer opinions. You offer observations to keep the flow going, and questions to spark further conversation, but no opinions. (Related to that, the interview is an opportunity to find out what the subject knows, not to impress him with what you know. Your subject is center stage right now. Keep him in the spotlight, and keep you out of it.)

Respect the source's time by not posing questions you could have answered before the interview began. Don't ask the mayor of your city how long she's been in office; that's something of an insult, and the mayor is going to wonder what other stupid questions might await her. This is especially true of celebrities who have given hundreds and maybe thousands of interviews. Ava Gardner once said of reporters: "They always ask the same questions. 'Tell us about Sinatra. Tell us about dancing on the tables.' God, don't they have any imagination at all?"

Try to keep the tone of the interview friendly, but don't let friendliness get in the way of the business at hand. For instance, allow the source to speak his mind, but don't give him license to wander away from the subject. Politely but firmly interrupt and ask questions that keep the conversation on track ("Let's come back to this topic later. We were talking about the start of your career before. Were you intimidated by the obstacles that faced you when you were starting out?").

Taking the Fifth

Remember at all points during your interviews (and other research, for that matter) that aggressiveness and obnoxiousness in theory are two different things. In practice, theory gives way to the zeal of would-be muckrakers who hound their sources and chastise them for not speaking for the record. As *Writer's Digest* columnist Art Spikol has frequently pointed out, no one *must* speak to you. Yes, the Constitution grants you the right to say and write whatever you want, but that same Constitution grants other people the right to keep their mouths shut. If someone you want to speak to exercises that right, respect it. Do what you can to reasonably talk the source into granting you an interview. Argue that the information will help other people, that it will help you present a balanced story, that you'd like to get it directly. Coax, but don't harass and harangue. And never claim that the source is obligated to speak to you.

If the source agrees to talk to you, but refuses to answer a specific question, use the same tactics. Or simply rephrase the question and use another angle to get your answer. But don't push, and don't pressure.

Pose touchy questions as a devil's advocate. Don't use the questions to attack your interviewee. An interview is rarely a confrontation, no matter how many times you've watched *60 Minutes*. And you are an interviewer, not a persecutor. Yes, don't shy away from the touchy questions, but phrase them delicately. If you want to discuss, for instance, certain indiscretions, say "I've heard from other sources that you often drive quite recklessly on your way to your job on the safety commission," not "Can you explain to me why you drive so recklessly. . . ."

Understand the meaning of the phrases "off the record," "not for publication," and "deep background": they mean that you can't use what the source is telling you. "Not for attribution" means you can use it, but you can't say who told you. Books can be and have been written about this topic. Consult those books (again, refer to the bibliography of this book) for more on the topic. My point here is that you should respect your source's wishes should he use one of these phrases.

Keeping Time

Honor the time limit that you set when arranging the interview. Note that your time is up, and that you're going to let the subject get back to work, or whatever. If he wants to continue chatting, the interview will move ahead by his choice, not because of your inconsiderateness.

At the end of the interview, ask permission to get back to the subject should you have further questions. Also, leave your business card (or jot down your address and phone number) in case the source wants to reach you with additional thoughts or information.

AFTER THE INTERVIEW

Something that many writers consider—incorrectly—a courtesy is agreeing to show the source your story before you submit it. Such a review can be helpful: the source can verify that your facts are correct (which can be especially reassuring if you're writing on a technical subject). But it also opens you up to "editing" by the source. "I didn't really say that—can we change it? And that section over here—how about if we just drop it?" This relinquishes quite a bit of power to the source, and can make things sticky when you choose to print something that the source said but later retracted when reviewing your manuscript. The source made the statement on the record; you have every right to print it. But, here again is an area best covered in other books. The point here, in the context of courtesy and professionalism, is that showing the source the completed manuscript prior to publication is not a courtesy. When a source asks to see the story, say that you're on a tight deadline and won't have time to show it. Better yet, just say no and explain that it's against general journalistic policies.

This doesn't mean that you *can't* show the story to the source if you want to. The choice is up to you.

Do send a copy of the published work to your sources. You needn't send the finished product—that could get awfully expensive if you have written a book. Simply photocopy the section of the book that your source helped you with. If you have written a magazine piece, you might as well photocopy the entire article, so that the source has a clear idea of how his comments or information fit in. Sending such copies is more than a simple courtesy, because it a) establishes you as a professional, and makes the source even more willing to cooperate with you on your next project, and b) satisfies the source's curiosity (though appearing in print may be common for you, it's doubtful that the source can say the same thing—besides, such mentions can elevate your source's professional standing and credibility, so of course he wants a copy to show off to his colleagues).

There's no need to send a copy to a source who answered only a couple of questions. But if he spent more than a half hour of his day for you, be considerate enough to demonstrate that the time was well spent.

If you consulted numerous sources, getting copies to all might be impractical. Use your discretion in such a case, but by no means overlook those who really went out of their way to help you. People accustomed to dispensing information—librarians and PR people, for instance—probably won't be hurt if you don't send copies to them. Consider sending copies anyway, to ensure future cooperation.

Do whatever you can to keep your sources happy. They deserve respect and gratitude, yes, and that is reason enough to deal with them courteously. But remember that they too are part of that publishing team that works together to communicate with readers, and should be treated accordingly.

10

The Most Important Words in the Professional Writer's Vocabulary

I don't have to tell you, a writer, about the power of words. And I don't have to tell you, the child of parents obsessed with politeness (and with telling you about it), about the importance of two specific English phrases: *please* and *thank you*. They're as important in this business as they are in any other realm, professional or social, that you function in.

Please is self-explanatory, and I'll leave it to you to use as you, um, please, except to say that used injudiciously, this word can lend a note of pleading to your requests ("May I please have the assignment?" is so much more shrill than "May I have the assignment?"). It can also convey exasperation and impatience ("Will you please send my check as soon as possible?" has an edge that "Will you send my check as soon as possible?" doesn't).

Thank you, on the other hand, needs a bit of discussion because there are so many ways to communicate gratitude in this business. Some of those ways are common and accepted and encouraged; some must be handled delicately.

Most used, of course, is the common courtesy of the verbal *thank you*. Say thanks as frequently as you would in other pursuits—

85

that is, whenever someone extends you a courtesy, a favor, a kindness. In the publishing business, that could be when an editor returns your call, after you've completed an interview with a source, and so on.

SPECIAL THANKS

If you're particularly grateful, follow up with a more tangible way of saying thank you: a phone call, a card or note, a gift. These methods have more impact than a verbal thanks because you must go out of your way to generate them, and the recipient appreciates that.

Of these methods, the card or note is generally the most appropriate. It doesn't bring into question your motives, as a gift might. And it can be passed around to other people, where a phone call cannot. The ability to share a note is important if, for instance, you are thanking the editor you worked closely with, yet you know that other editors helped out and deserve recognition.

Phone call or note or both, keep it brief, and, more important, sincere. Don't gush. Here's a sample of a thank-you note that I think is simple, dignified, and effective. I received it after I bought a manuscript that had gone through a couple of revisions, and I appreciated it. "Glad to hear my story will work for you. Thanks for all the effort *you* have put into this piece. I'm looking forward to seeing author's galleys."

If you're thanking an information source, drop a note into the mail shortly after the interview, then jot another note when you send along a copy of the published work. Be especially dutiful in sending that copy. (You can ask editors to send you extra copies that you can mail to sources, or ask if they will send copies directly to the sources if you supply names and addresses. Often editors will accommodate such requests.)

The Art of Gift-Giving

Within reason, a gift to editors or agents—sometimes even a source—is acceptable. But those gifts should be a sincere gesture of gratitude, and not bribes of any sort. The only bribe you can give editors that will entice them to publish your manuscript is an excellent manuscript. Bribe them with publishable writing, and you will be published.

Congratulatory gifts are always acceptable: a bottle of champagne to an editor after the book the two of you worked so hard and long on comes off the press, for example. One author sent homemade fudge to the Writer's Digest Books editorial department after her book came out.

Gifts for condolence are appropriate: for example, flowers to an editor you've worked with who has lost a loved one.

Of course, Christmas cards and the like are perfectly acceptable. In fact, many people and companies send cards during the holiday season as a regular business practice, to keep their names in front of the people they conduct business with.

And everyone appreciates congratulatory notes and cards commemorating a special event in a person's life (the birth of a child, a wedding, a birthday). If you are in a position to know about such events in the first place, you obviously know that person well enough that cards and greetings could in no way be interpreted as anything less than sincere.

To sum up, gifts are appropriate if they are: heartfelt, inexpensive, something the recipient would enjoy seeing or using (writers occasionally send me baseball or pinball doodads because of my interest in those hobbies), and given to someone you've worked closely with, someone who won't be uncomfortable with or offended by a gift. Remember, though, that most times a brief, sincere note will accomplish as much as a gift, and usually more.

Remember, too, that few established pros give gifts with any frequency. Therefore, there's a certain zeal associated with such a gesture that can smack of exuberant amateurism.

Thanks in Print

Books offer you another way to say thanks: the acknowledgments page. Here you can list everyone who gave you a hand with the project—from sources to family members to editors to proofreaders to the local librarians. You can even explain the exact nature of the help, and throw in a few compliments and/or personal comments. Believe me, the acknowledgments page won't be the best-read part of the book, but here you're concerned with only a select group of readers: those you have chosen to honor by devoting a page to them. This is different from the dedication page. Generally, you acknowledge help on that specific book, while you dedicate the book to someone who has played an important part in your life. But the acknowledgments and dedication pages are your business; write on them what you will.

Check published books in your library to see how their authors handled acknowledgments and dedications. This book contains one of each, and they appear before the introduction.

And, of course, when your book hits the bestseller list and you put in your appearance on the Carson show, you can voice your thanks in front of a national audience.

ONE MORE PHRASE YOUR PARENTS DRILLED INTO YOU THAT BEARS REPEATING

Finally, remember the importance of *I'm sorry.* "I'm sorry the article is late," "I'm sorry that one of the interviews I told you I'd include fell through," and so on. If you've made a blunder or a mistake or whatever, acknowledge it, explain it (but don't make excuses), and apologize. Then get on with your business.

Thanks.

11

The Diplomacy of Disagreement: Arguments, Negotiations, and Complaints

Let me paraphrase a sign that I've seen too often: "Rule #1—The Editor Is Always Right. Rule #2—When the Editor is Wrong, See Rule #1."

Well, I've not heard of many magazines where that's always true (of course, that rule *always* applies at the magazine *I* edit). Editors are not always right. There are times when you will disagree with them, when you'll want to negotiate with them for better deals, when you'll get out-and-out ticked off and want to blow off steam. You have every right to do so.

Editors and agents don't welcome disagreement, but they understand that few dealings won't encounter some difference in point of view somewhere along the line. They are prepared to negotiate, to discuss, and sometimes to argue.

In fact, disagreements are on the rare occasion even encouraged. Sometimes you have more than the right to disagree. You have the obligation to do so. If you find that you can say, "I'm sorry, but the slant you suggest is misleading," you *must* say it. If you

89

could say, "You might want to reconsider your plans for the book because I can't possibly deliver a full-length manuscript by your deadline," say it.

If you find yourself dissatisfied with something—payment, the way you've been treated, the copyediting of your manuscript—use these negotiating guidelines to resolve the situation. The tips apply to clearing up potential problems and disagreements early in your relationship with an editor (if, for example, you want to request that the editor pay your expenses on the assignment you're about to begin working on), and to resolving arguments and complaints after problems have arisen (if, for example, you don't agree with the title the publisher wants to give your novel).

Recognize the potential for negotiation in the first place. I once made an assignment to an author who balked because he thought my payment was too low, and that I was offering to devote too little space to the story (I wanted 1,500 words; he wanted to write 3,000). Instead of negotiating for a higher fee and more space, he refused the assignment. As I wrote him: "I hope you'll remember that these offers aren't take-'em-or-leave-'em. This one could have been a let's-talk-about-'em-until-we-get-something-we're-both-happy-with."

When an editor comes to you with an offer that is less than what you'd be happy with, don't take offense, don't take umbrage. No offense is intended in a businesslike offer that reflects what the editor believes she can buy something for. If she can't buy it for that price, let her know—and let her know what the price *is*. "There's nothing wrong with a writer simply saying he can't do a certain piece for the money offered," says Greg Daugherty of *Sylvia Porter's Personal Finance*. "That gives the editor two options: either trying to improve the fee (though editors probably have less leeway with fees than writers suspect) or looking for another writer." An offer is a hand extended—with the eventual goal of a handshake when the deal is closed, not with the goal of slapping your face.

Try to eliminate the possibility of disagreement at the outset. The earlier you identify potential problems, the better. I once got cranky with a writer who queried us on a 1,000-word article. We gave him the assignment, and offered $100, our standard payment for an article of that length by an author we haven't worked with before. When he submitted the piece, he wrote, "Here's the article, but I won't sell it to you for less than $200." I'll never work with that author again. If he had problems with our offered payment, he should have requested more money *before* beginning work on the article. "Once a writer has agreed to do a piece, there's no point trying to make the editor feel guilty about the terms," says Greg Daugherty. "I had a writer say to me once, 'You know, the money you're paying me is criminal.' I haven't made him an accessory to any such crimes since then."

Make sure everyone involved understands any agreements, financial or otherwise, at the very outset, and get everything in writing. If an editor gives you an assignment, but hasn't mentioned how much you'll be paid, ask. Similarly, make sure the editor has stated the magazine's policy about a kill fee, deadline, length of the completed manuscript, the need for photos and/or illustrations, and so on. Make sure that statement appears in a letter somewhere, so you can file it. If you're writing a book, all such matters will be spelled out clearly in the contract (no book deals are made verbally)—if they're not spelled out, be wary. For more advice on these matters, consult Richard Balkin's *How to Understand & Negotiate a Book Contract or Magazine Agreement* (see the bibliography for details).

Similarly, anticipate and head off problems as early as possible. For example, you might ask to see a copy-edited manuscript before it goes to the typesetter, instead of seeing author's galleys of the typeset manuscript. Correcting editing that you don't agree with is far less expensive before the manuscript is set than it is after. Or, to avoid conflict over the title of a story or book, ask that the editor give you a list of the titles the publisher is considering. Better yet, if you suspect that the editor might change the title, offer your own list.

Assume nothing. For instance, if an editor asks you to ship him something via overnight mail, he will generally reimburse you. But don't assume that he will. Ask if you will indeed be reimbursed.

If you conduct business on the phone, especially if specific dollar amounts are discussed or if any commitment is made to you (such as an assignment), follow up with a letter that both parties can file. For example, "This is to confirm our phone conversation Thursday, in which we agreed to a $350 fee for a 2,000-word article, due Sept. 9."

Alert your editor to problems, potential or otherwise, as soon as you identify them. Say you're writing an article, and the editor has agreed to pay your expenses. But you encounter more costs than you had expected, and the expense bill seems to be ballooning. Warn the editor, and ask if she will cover the increased expenses. Don't surprise the editor later on with a huge bill.

Air out your concerns as soon as possible, even if the concerns don't apply to specific problems. There are times when you will sense that a vague sort of "trouble" is brewing, that your relationship with your agent or editor is deteriorating. When this happens, discuss it openly with whoever's involved. I once made a joke in a letter to a writer I've worked with for a number of years. He didn't see it as a joke, and his next letter was rather defensive. I didn't waste any time getting to the phone to clear matters up. Especially when a miscommunication is involved, a phone call can be more effective than a letter because of its immediacy, and because you can talk back and forth until both of you understand exactly what's going on. Another of my regular writers was dismayed about the fact that I had been slow in responding to him about one of his projects. We exchanged letters about the subject, and I thought everything was squared away. It wasn't. The writer called one morning and said, "That delay isn't typical of our relationship, and I wanted to talk to you about it, and to see if anything's wrong." We did indeed talk, and we brought up some mutual concerns and settled them and generally reestablished our relationship. I was happy for the opportunity to clear up some misunderstandings, and I appreciated the writer's respect for our working relationship.

Ask yourself honestly if the problem is something you can do anything about, or if it is something you have any say over. Just as editors aren't always right, they aren't always wrong, either. Sometimes quibbling simply won't do any good. The focus and slant of a manuscript is one such area. You may want to write me an author profile that concentrates on his use of word processing, and I may want you to write a profile that focuses on the author's use of transitions in fiction. In this situation, I'm right. You make two mistakes when you question an editor's decision about his magazine, especially when it concerns the slant of a story, the information a manuscript should contain, or (as I'll discuss later) whether the manuscript is at all suitable for the publication in the first place. First, you're apt to be wrong. How could your perspective of the magazine and its audience be better than that of someone who is intimate with the magazine eight or more hours a day? Second, you're apt to insult the editor by implying he doesn't know his own magazine or—worse yet—doesn't care about it.

Of course, you do have some say in the matter. If you want to focus on word processing in the profile, you can withdraw the idea from me and sell it to someone else.

Book writers have more leeway in this matter of slant, because the length of the project and the fact that a book is a self-contained unit (while a magazine article is but a part of the whole of the publication) combine to give the author more autonomy. But these basic principles apply to both magazine articles and books:

• If you and the editor disagree before an assignment is made or a contract signed, you can take your work to another editor.

• If you disagree after the assignment or contract is finalized, you risk having the manuscript rejected. In book publishing, you may find the "unacceptable manuscript" clause of your contract invoked against you. This clause obligates you to producing a manuscript acceptable to the publisher. If you don't, you risk not only rejection, but also being required to return the advance.

This is not to say that you should do *everything* the editor requests. As I'll discuss in a moment, almost anything is open to negotiation. But in terms of this discussion, remember that there are some things you have control over, and some that you don't.

Don't take criticism or revision suggestions personally. Your writing is a vehicle, a means of communication. If it doesn't communicate, it must be reworked until it does. But there's more to it than that: the fact that the writing must be reworked according to *one person's* conception of communication. That person is the editor. She has certain ideas about what the writing should accomplish *in the context of the magazine she publishes or the book lists she puts together*. In other words, magazines and book publishers have certain personalities that result from the personality of the editor, the personality of the publisher, and the personalities of the readers. Much editing is done to allow an individual manuscript to fit in with that personality, and to conform to reader demands. Yes, editors want to retain the author's voice as much as possible—as long as doing that serves the reader. Editors aren't asking you for revisions to insult you; they are trying to please the reader.

And as a side note, respect yourself enough to allow yourself the occasional failure. Don't get depressed when your manuscript just plain doesn't work, and is rejected. I spoke before of Isaac Asimov who, when writing an article for me, said he wouldn't take a kill fee if he didn't deliver a publishable manuscript. He expected that he might encounter failure, not necessarily in the project he was going to write for me, but *sometime*, at some point in his career. He was prepared for it. And unafraid of it. Just as a professional should be.

Of course, you can't consider the editor's returning your manuscript for rewrite as failure.

Try to understand why the person you're negotiating with is taking the stand she is, and use that to your benefit. Don't discuss the stance itself; discuss the reason behind the stance. Acknowledge it, then offer alternatives that address the actual problem. Suppose, for instance, you want to see prepublication galleys of your magazine article, but the editor is reluctant to send them to you. Ask yourself why. Maybe she's worried that showing you author's galleys adds another step to the production schedule, therefore slowing the process. Tell the editor: "To make sure that my review of author's galleys doesn't delay you, I promise one-day turnaround (for a magazine piece—one or two weeks for a book), and I will respond via Express Mail or by phone if you prefer." Or maybe the editor fears that you will object to how the manuscript was edited, or that you will make—and demand—extensive changes. Tell her: "I understand how costly it can be to make corrections once a manuscript has been typeset, so I will be looking at the galleys primarily to make sure that spellings are right and facts are accurate and up-to-date. I will keep author's corrections to a minimum."

As another example, a writer once argued a small change we had made in his manuscript. He said that the change made a sentence sound too formal, and could we please change it back? He ignored the fact that the change corrected a grammatical gaffe. Since he offered us no alternative that corrected both the grammar and the slight shift in tone, we were forced to correct the more substantive problem. Our change stood.

If you don't understand the editor's position, ask him to explain it. This will give you ammunition for winning your argument, as I explained above, or it could show you that the editor is indeed right.

Use a friendly tone and humor when broaching a disagreement.
Alex Heard is a writer who used humor to ask that I bump his payment: "My mother says you should pay me more so I can afford to get her the new matching socks she's been wanting, but it's not my style to saddle editors with 'guilt' and whatnot." I laughed, and he got his money. (He wrote back: "Thanks. I promise I won't beg again until next time.") Keep in mind, though, that Heard was more able to use this gambit because we had already established a friendly working relationship over the couple of years we'd been working together. Humor can be a little touchier with editors you haven't worked with for a while. Still, no matter what the length of the working relationship, it's always wise to be pleasant throughout your dealings with editors.

Remember that standing your ground doesn't communicate disrespect, and that backing off doesn't necessarily communicate respect. Taking a firm stance on an issue—whether a payment policy or some copyediting you'd like changed back to the original—will not offend an editor. Arrogance, shrillness, indignation, and other posturing while taking the stance will.

Present your case calmly. Persuade, don't push and provoke. Don't argue emotionally. Argue as if you were an objective third party. Use logic, not exclamation points and printed shouts of "for shame" to make your point.

Avoid verbal jousting. It's such an easy trap for a writer, proud of his verbal abilities, to fall into when he's frustrated or angered by something. Insults, no matter how clever, get you nowhere. Sarcasm, swipes, cheap shots, smartass remarks—all get you the same place. We once ran a contest inviting brief commentaries about language and word use. One of the entrants clipped out the item I had written to announce the contest and pointed out several imagined and a couple of (I admit) real gaffes in the text. Did he really expect to win the contest that way? That's smartass, and it got him a little further than nowhere. It got him rejected.

If someone else should level the first attack at you, resist the urge to respond in kind. What's the point? I once received an indignant letter claiming that I wasn't willing to devote three or four pages to a profile of a specific writer because my magazine spent so much space telling readers how to describe the heroine's lips in confession stories or somesuch hoo-ha. In a moment of weakness, and feeling my pride in my work being hurt, I wrote back something to the effect that maybe we should have published the suggested profile, except that we were all booked up with pieces profiling Kurt Vonnegut, Ray Bradbury, Joyce Carol Oates, and the authors of *Inherit the Wind*, all of whom discussed how to describe the heroine's lips in confession stories in great detail. What did I gain? I never should have degraded myself by mailing that letter. It changed nothing.

Here's another good reason to restrain yourself: what if you level a brilliant verbal attack and later find out that you're wrong? When the editor or whoever comes back and politely points out that you're wrong, it's going to be difficult to write that letter of apology. But if you are indeed wrong, admit it. Demonstrate that you have the character to do so.

Suggest, don't demand.   You will find more support if you offer to work together to solve problems and disagreements than if you offer ultimatums. The letter from Alex Heard requesting more money so he could buy his mom new matching socks suggested higher payment instead of demanding it.

Don't approach the subject defensively, as if you are expecting trouble.   That's a self-fulfilling prophecy. Remember the writer I talked about in Chapter 1 who begged me not to get my dander up, and my dander went up anyway? Avoid phrasings like "I know you're not going to like this" or "Why don't you try to be reasonable?" or anything else that would make the editor think "Oh oh, what's coming next?" when she reads it.

Argue confidently, but not pretentiously.   No one likes dealing with prima donnas. "I've had 450 articles published in magazines across the country," a writer will argue, "which proves I know exactly what I'm doing, so you must not change a word in my article." As an editor, I'm not worried about the 450 articles. I'm worried about *this one*. I'm not worried about the writer's ego. I'm worried about my readers' trust in me to present articles they will enjoy and benefit from.

Choose your battles carefully.   If you argue too often, the editor will simply brand you as argumentative—being difficult for the sake of being difficult—and start to ignore you. There's also the "cry wolf" factor involved, so start shouting only when you really mean it. Besides, some matters are insignificant; your time and energy are better spent elsewhere. For example, give in to editing changes made for what's known as "house style"—the prescribed way to spell certain words, etc. *Writer's Digest* spells out all numbers under 11, while numbers up to 100 (including eleven) are spelled out in this book. These are matters of the differences between the style of the magazine division and the book division—"style" being a list of preferred ways to spell words and punctuate sentences and so on, with a goal of making each reference consistent with all others. Sure, you may want to spell the word as *grey* in your manuscript, because it communicates the feeling of the color more than the same word spelled with an *a*, but the magazine's style dictates *gray*. Ultimately, this is inconsequential. Don't argue over it. Editors dig in over matters of house style—it's one of their peculiarities.

Remember that although negotiation and other dealings are sometimes adversarial relationships, they are not fist fights. Negotiation is a matter of give and.take, not punch and feint. Therefore, leave bitterness, snideness, sarcasm, rancor, name-calling, and snippetiness out of it. If you negotiate, argue, even complain with composure, respect, and professionalism, the person you're dealing with will respond in kind. For example, a while back I wrote a feature for a Sunday newspaper magazine. The day it appeared, my wife brought in the paper and said, "You won't like this." I didn't know what she meant; I liked the splashy layout my editor had given the story, and I loved the huge four-color photos that accompanied it. But I didn't like the byline. It said, "by Jim Brohaugh." And all these years my Mom had called me Bill. Well, I could have written a nasty note impugning proofreaders and castigating typesetters and questioning the sanity and competence of editors. That note would have gained me nothing. Instead, I wrote the editor a letter expressing exactly what I felt. "I liked the layout and the photos a lot," I wrote. "I think the whole story was presented smashingly. That's why I'm all the more disappointed that somehow I became Jim in the byline. Any idea how that happened?" I then asked for— and eventually received—an editor's note in a succeeding issue correcting the mistake. My request was probably granted of the editor's obligation to me, but the fact that I didn't scream in his ear like a bear more indignant than seriously wounded by a hunter's shot didn't hurt.

Editors don't like misunderstandings, and they don't like to make mistakes. If you point out mistakes to them, their pride will eat at them; you don't have to eat at them, too. Mistakes are not made on purpose. Work to correct the mistake, not to make a fool of the person who made it.

Don't accuse anyone of intentionally doing something seemingly senseless until you're sure that an honest mistake was not the culprit. I've seen instances when important words have been deleted from a story in going from manuscript copy to galleys; the author, when seeing the galleys, ranted on about the "stupid" copyediting when the deletion was simply a typographical error.

Likewise, don't complain unless you are sure of yourself. Don't, for instance, accuse a copy editor of ignorantly inserting an extra *a* into *camraderie* or an extra *m* into *accomodate*, as writers have done to our copy editors, until you have checked. *Camaraderie* and *accommodate* may look wrong, but they're correct.

Don't blame someone when it will do you no good. If something has gone wrong, ask yourself if finger-pointing will do you or the situation any good. If it won't, let it pass. I worked with one author over a period of a couple of years on a story. In a letter about it, the author wrote me, "It has to be my longest-running article assignment; thanks for your patience." To tell the truth, that article hit as many delays on my end as on hers . . . and she's thanking *me* for *my* patience.

Keep outsiders out of it. The negotiation is between you and the person you're negotiating with. The president of your writing circle may think you deserve better, but such testimony is a flimsy negotiating lever. Explain why *you* think you deserve better. Back that opinion with evidence of your professional stature, or with arguments about what you will invest in the project that warrants the treatment you seek.

Point to the policies of other magazines or publishers only if *you* are accustomed to benefitting from those policies. If you're negotiating with a sports magazine, for instance, don't say, "*Sports Illustrated* would pay $1,000 for that type of story." Perhaps for that *type* of story, but would *Sports Illustrated* pay that much for your story specifically? And if it would, why not sell it there? At least, that's what the editor you're negotiating with will ask you.

On the other hand, if you can say, "I've been writing this type of story for sports magazines for some years now, and my typical fee is $1,000," do it. This establishes a track record not so much in terms of specific payment, but in terms of the fact that other editors have been willing to make that payment, presumably because the quality of your work warrants it. It also implies that you can afford to break off negotiations and take your services elsewhere—establishing your position of strength.

Don't beg, and don't plead financial hardship. Don't try to make the editor feel guilty. Resorting to such ploys is undignified. Don't argue that you need the money, or whatever it is that you're seeking. Argue that you *deserve* it.

Demonstrate how granting your request will benefit the project at hand. "A larger advance will allow me to devote more time to the book in the next six months, allowing me more travel time to conduct interviews that will give the book greater depth." Or, "Allowing me to see author's galleys will give you an extra set of proofreading eyes, which will help ensure that the article goes into print error-free."

Demonstrate how granting your request will benefit the editor or publisher. "A larger advance will allow me the extra time to include an appendix profiling a major industry organization involved with the subject of my book. If we include that, we could get a lot of free promotion within the organization." Or, "Sending me twenty-five free contributor's copies of the magazine instead of ten will allow me to distribute copies to some of my contacts within the field, including a couple of newspaper book critics, which will increase the visibility of the magazine."

Go over the head of the person you're dealing with only as a last resort, and only if you can live with the working relationship ending there. If you can't get what you want from the editor you've been working with—a check, for instance—go to her superior: a superior editor, or the publisher. But realize that the editor won't appreciate such a move, as it's drawing fire to her. Tough luck, you may say, and you're right. But just don't expect that editor to be eager to work with you again.

Threaten legal measures only if you have some legal base to do so, and, again, as a last resort that will likely burn the last of the bridges. If you hit the point where you think lawyers and judges and such will enter the picture—say, to secure payment for a manuscript used but never paid for, or for breach of a book contract—you are past the point of mere etiquette, and your situation is outside of the scope of this book.

Use the bluff as a negotiating tactic judiciously. If you say, "Unless we can agree on a figure of $500 for this piece, I won't be able to do it," be prepared for the consequences. Better to say something to the effect of "A $500 fee will be important to my approaching the assignment with the enthusiasm needed to make the article really shine." The latter sentence is firm, yet leaves room for negotiating.

Stand by yourself. If you find that you can't give in to the other party for whatever reason—financial, ethical, practical—don't. Simply explain your reasoning and, if you can, back away from the project. If the problem cropped up at a late stage, and you are obliged to finish the work, fulfill your obligation. But see what you can do to disassociate yourself from it. For instance, if you are truly embarrassed by how your article has been copyedited, and you can't coax the editor to overrule the copyediting, you might ask that the piece appear without your byline. If the damage is already done—if your byline has appeared in print as Jim and your name is Bill, register your complaint and then forget it. Move on to the next project. Don't stew. Don't become so preoccupied that a single problem causes problems in unrelated projects.

And don't succumb to the parting shot, or any other sort of bridge-burning. I've had people refuse to write for me because they felt they deserved more money than I was budgeted to pay. Some of those people felt compelled to insult me. I've not worked with them again. Others simply said something to the effect of "I think it's wiser for me to work on projects that will net me more income," said thank you and bowed out. In at least one case, I was able to return to one of the latter writers and work out an assignment—after I had been allocated a bigger editorial budget.

Besides, editors move from magazine to magazine and publisher to publisher, where rates and policies could differ. The editor you're snubbing at *Backhoe Weekly* might one day find himself on the staff of *Playboy*.

Don't burn your bridges. You just might want to cross them again.

12

The Bizarre World of "Rejecting" Rejection

Perhaps the most memorable correspondence I've been involved with in my years at *Writer's Digest* involved an editor who freelanced on the side. He queried us on a topic we liked, and we gave him the assignment. When the manuscript came in, we found it just a rant or two short of raving; it was too one-sided to be useful. We asked the author for a rewrite, but he refused—for no apparent reason. That was strike one against him.

This same author proposed another article—a potentially controversial one—but this time gave us only a topic. When we asked for more information, he sent us a carbon of another article on the same topic that he had written for a magazine for *nurses*. "I'll write the same article for you," he wrote, "only aimed at writers." I asked myself, If he's too lazy to type a page of information tailored to my magazine, what kind of ambition will he exhibit when it comes to the article itself? Strike two, the umpire called. We rejected the idea.

Then, I got . . . well, I got something that I love to use as a visual aid when I talk about this incident at writers conferences: My rejection letter, crumpled, torn almost in half, with—I swear—teeth marks near the bottom. An accompanying note, uncrumpled, untorn, untoothed, said: "Let's not sully *Writers Digest* with realism, no no. When are you going to send me my kill fee for the first article so we can bring all of this to a deserved close?" Well—strike three, obviously, and not just because he had misspelled the name of my magazine. Not just because he was rude. But because he had shown himself to be a rank amateur by "rejecting" my rejection. The moral of the story—in terms of what I've been saying about ending up on the editor's blacklist—is revealed by what I found strangest of all: the writer came to bat again. That's right. Not long after he had insulted me, made figurative obscene gestures at me, he queried me with another idea. I did not consider the query; I refused even to read it.

I've received my share of "wounded puppy" letters from rejected authors ("How could you have? I was *sure* that my article/ poem/*screenplay* was perfect for your magazine. . . ."), but this was a series of wounded bear letters. And as any outdoorsman will happily tell you, there are two things you never do with wounded bears: 1) Mess around with them. 2) Buy manuscripts from them.

I encounter writers who question or argue or debate a decision to return an article on almost a daily basis. One book editor I know refers to these writers as "The Unrejectables." As she says, "Some unrejectables *resubmit* their manuscripts every six months or so . . . the same manuscripts."

It's OK to get angry over rejection. As writer Lawrence Block says, "You'd be a bit loony if you didn't." But, as Block also says, "Get angry, then forget about it." Don't dwell on it. And don't express your anger to editors. Pros don't yell and scream. In general, respect editors and trust them with what is, after all, *their* job. With that in mind:

Don't berate the editor or the magazine for not seeing the worth of the submission, or worse yet, imply that the editor doesn't know what he's doing. Don't call him dim, or apathetic, or incompetent, or short-sighted. Remember that he holds that position for several reasons, and dimness, apathy, incompetence, and short-sightedness probably aren't among them.

Particularly amateurish is the accusation that the editor declined because he fears giving a new creative voice a chance, or because he fears peering out of a cozy, well-appointed rut. More than one writer has claimed that I had rejected a manuscript because I was unwilling to take risks with my readers. Well, there are three arguments against that. First, few editors want to get too daring. I'd be willing to be the first to concede that, if hundreds of editors before me hadn't already made this concession. Readers pick up a magazine expecting it to provide certain types of information and/or entertainment. Editors seek to fulfill those expectations. If they get too daring, they lose readers. Second, all editors do take certain risks; we want to surprise the reader every once in a while. But it's our job to determine which risks and which surprises are reasonable. Third, we're *always* eager to find new creative voices. That accusation is flat-out wrong.

Besides, the editors are in the best position to determine what is fresh, because we have seen everything that isn't. One writer queried me on a story about filing systems for writers. After I turned her down, she wrote back to me, "The problem with your magazine is that it refuses to strike out into bold new directions." Filing systems is a bold new direction?

Don't ask the editor to reconsider a rejection because he or she "missed the point." Editors are as capable of missing a point as anyone else, I'll admit, but the plain fact of the matter is that your manuscript was probably rejected for some reason not related to point-missing.

Don't go over the first reader's head and ask a superior editor to consider the submission. Yes, first readers make mistakes. They can overlook something that could work perfectly well for the magazine or turn into a strong seller for the book publisher. Senior editors, though, can make the same mistakes. So don't look at the first readers as a bunch of know-nothing obstacles. I once received a manuscript (labeled "Personal" on the outside envelope) accompanied by this letter: "I just got this manuscript back with a rejection note from your assistant editor. I don't think the assistant understood the query, so I thought it important that you see it." I glanced at it, but pretty much rejected it out of hand, for the reasons I told him—first, our assistant editor serves as the reader because she is good at the job, and second, the first reader is an important position, which we tried to fill with someone whose judgment we trusted. As I wrote to the author: "We have a good reason for following the review procedure your manuscript was subjected to. It works."

Don't accuse the editor of not having read the submission. First of all, so what if he hasn't? He has no obligation to read everything that comes in. Don't get me wrong. I believe that editors should conscientiously and fairly consider all submissions made in good faith, and if they aren't going to, they should announce their policy as widely as possible. But in the rare case where an editor hasn't read a submission, he has likely not done so for a reason he feels is justified, a reason that you aren't going to convince him is wrong (the subject was recently covered in his magazine, or four misspellings appear on the first page). Again, you're not going to change his mind.

Second, what evidence would conclusively demonstrate that he hasn't read it? You can't dust the first few pages for prints.

Third, you risk making a fool of yourself, especially if the editor has indeed read your submission. I've received letters accusing me of not having read a previously submitted query letter. Now, if that were true, if I truly refused to read letters, why would the writer think I would read the letter accusing me of not reading letters?

We most often receive these accusations if we respond quickly to submissions, so:

Don't quibble about how quickly the manuscript was returned. We try to deal with submissions the day they arrive, and writers get angry when we respond *too quickly*. They claim that we couldn't have given their manuscripts proper consideration in such a short time, as if aging the manuscripts on our desks for a couple of days would sharpen our judgment. And if you think that editors don't often receive such complaints, I offer the story of the major publisher whose first readers would set rejected manuscripts aside a week before returning them, just to deflect such criticism.

To so many topics and ideas we can say no before you have even finished the first sentence of your query, the first page of your manuscript. Yet, believe me: we have given the idea proper consideration. We have thought it through. We didn't just begin thinking about it at the moment you proposed it to us. We began last week, last month, last year. We have discussed if not that idea then at least similar ones dozens of times in editorial meetings. Or we've thought of the idea ourselves but decided against it. Or we ran something similar years ago and It Just Didn't Work then, and It Just Won't Work now. Some decisions may seem spur-of-the-moment to you, but that particular moment started a long time ago for us. We may have talked about your specific idea, about similar ideas, about the category your idea falls into.

Don't revise and resubmit a rejected manuscript if the editor has

explained why it was rejected unless the editor specifically asks to see it again. Many editors try to explain why they are rejecting a piece, but that bit of kindness can backfire if the writer turns around and submits a revised version. The spirit is admirable. But the fact remains that if the editor wants you to revise the manuscript for him, he will ask you, directly and specifically, to do it.

Don't ask the editor why something was rejected if no reason was given you. Sometimes there *was* no reason. "The phrase is a familiar one in rejection letters written to agents and authors in response to submissions: 'We don't feel the book would be right for our list,' " write James Wade and Richard Marek in *Editors on Editing*. "Well, there is in that stock phrase a lot of collective experience, intelligent guesswork, and honest admission of incapability to see the right way to publish the book." Other times, the reason is a matter of one person's opinion, which other editors you submit the piece to won't necessarily share. You would be tempted to alter your manuscript based on one reader's opinion. The one opinion you should pay attention to at this point is yours.

Don't threaten to cancel your subscription because of a rejection. Cancel it if you want. But don't threaten to. Especially if you don't have one.

Don't point to something the magazine or publishing house has recently published and compare your rejected manuscript favorably to it. You may be right. Yours may be better. But don't expect the editor to slap himself on the forehead with the palm of his hand and exclaim, "By gosh you're right! I'll take it after all."

A related faux pas is clipping a recently published piece and sending it to the editor with the rejection slip you received attached to it. I admit that I once was tempted to do this. I wrote a humor piece that was rejected with a brief note: "Weak." I almost, almost clipped out some of that magazine's humor that I thought was weak, and almost, almost sent it to the editor with his note. I was much younger then. I recently ran across my copy of that humor piece, by the way. Know something? That thing—and I see this quite clearly now—was weak.

Don't send back a rejection slip after you have circled the typos and other errors. Granted, I've seen some atrociously prepared rejection slips in my day, with misspellings and grammatical errors and, in a couple of cases, the names of the magazines misspelled. You don't have to point those out to the people who rejected your work. The only one who will care about your implicit message ("No wonder you were so incompetent in rejecting my work; you can't even get a simple rejection slip right") is you. I won't apologize for such sloppiness, but I will point out that getting the rejection slip perfect is of a far lower priority than getting the magazine out on time, than getting the book to the typesetters on deadline.

Don't send back the rejection slip with a curt, cute note: "Sorry to have to return this rejection slip to you. It doesn't meet my needs at this time." Or, "I'm sorry, but I'm overstocked with similar material." Avoid this not because it's tacky (which it definitely is), but because it just ain't original.

Don't blast the editor with what one editor has called "snotty rhetorical questions." At *Writer's Digest*, we receive remarks like this from the occasional writer: "How could a magazine supposedly looking out for writers possibly send me a rejection slip?" Elizabeth Crow of *Parents* magazine says she sometimes gets return letters saying things like, "I had assumed that you were interested in safety for children." Says Crow: "They're trying to make you feel guilty. That's crude."

Don't gloat when your rejected manuscript finds the right editor. Says agent Evan Marshall: "At several conferences writers have approached me and told me that they were the ones who submitted proposals for such-and-such and I rejected them, and how could I be so rude (which my letters never are), or wouldn't I please reconsider, or 'I'm happy to inform you that I did find an agent who saw the merits of my work.' Unprofessional, unnecessary, futile, obnoxious."

Don't bother arguing a negative decision that is based purely on taste. We once rejected a batch of cartoons with the note, "Just didn't make enough of us laugh." The indignant cartoonist wrote back, first claiming that cartoons don't make people laugh; at most, they evoke a "gentle smile." (Can you see us rejecting something because it "just didn't make enough of us smile gently"?) Then he clipped out two cartoons that had appeared in a recent issue and jotted beside them, "If there is a laugh here, I couldn't find it." (I could; I laughed again at them—yes, aloud.) Just what do you think this cartoonist was trying to achieve? Was he trying to change my mind, or was he more ambitiously trying to "upgrade" my taste, my sense of humor? The second goal is impossible to achieve, and after I received his letter, so was his first.

In sum, please don't pour your anger about a rejection into a letter where it will splash out all over some editor only trying to do his job. Not only does this signal that you're rude and unprofessional, but it also implies that you're an unpleasant person—and who goes out of his way to work with unpleasant people?

But something far more important than the danger of putting off editors is at work here. Such reactions hurt more than your career. They hurt *you*. Please don't take rejection so personally that you feel you must argue with it. Such arguing—it's *fretting*, really— is a symptom of a defense mechanism at work, one that consumes time and energy, and consumes a little bit of you by exercising bitterness that is counterproductive at best. At worst, it's acidic.

The best way to argue a rejection—to that editor who rebuffed you, or, perhaps, to yourself—is to prove your material's worth. Sell it to another market. Sell it to a *competitor*. Arguing with the editor rarely gets you anywhere, except onto a list of writers that editor would rather not deal with. It's the editor's job to edit the magazine or design the book list, not yours. You are a contributor, not a consultant. Don't drive from the back seat; the view isn't all that good back there.

13

The Only Person Who Absolutely Deserves Your Respect and Courtesy

Editors and agents deserve your respect, your courtesy, just as any other human being does. But these people—as well as any other people in the publishing business, from typesetters to art directors to the postal employee who delivers your acceptances and rejections—have no reserved spot on any publishing pedestal. The only pedestal you should recognize—you *must* recognize—in this business supports the reader.

Readers are the only people who absolutely deserve respect and courtesy. You must respect them by not writing down to them and by not putting your artistic flights above their need for information and entertainment. In other words, whether you believe you're working for an editor, publisher, an agent, or yourself, you're really working for those persons who pick up your story looking for something that serves them.

Therefore, I have to revise a point I made earlier in this book: Ultimately, it *is* the writing that counts. Be faithful to the writing and to the people who read it. That's the ultimate in professional courtesy, and all the professional guidelines covered in this book are presented so that you can reach the point where you are allowed to demonstrate that ultimate.

To show your respect for those all-important readers:

Write to share, not lecture.   Point out what's interesting and useful, and withhold what's not. Include nothing that reflects *only* the thoroughness of your research; throw out anything that has the feel of a "see-what-I-know" boast.

Be a storyteller.   Even if you write nonfiction, your readers expect you to weave a tale—to present the information as compellingly as possible. Be considerate enough to fulfill their expectations.

Answer all your readers' questions before they get a chance to ask them.   Examine everything you write and ask yourself, Is this self-contained? Does it raise additional questions? Is it too general, which would leave readers craving specification or clarification, or is it maybe too detailed, leaving readers wondering why you were so exhaustive? Is the advice you give concrete and specific, allowing readers to put it to immediate use? Must readers dig further to put your advice to use?

Be honest with your readers.   Don't twist or mold facts to fit the story. The tiny lies that fall out during such twisting will accumulate into a monstrous—and deserved—lack of credibility.

Don't withhold facts, either by design or by failure to do proper research. And don't elevate any particular fact, event, or subject beyond its actual importance simply to make a story more interesting. In fact, work to put your subject in its proper perspective, not only in its world, but in the readers' world as well. Ask yourself, "What does this mean to my readers?" Then tell readers your answer.

Much of this depends on your motive in writing about your topic. To promote it? To satisfy your own interest in it? To benefit the reader? To benefit yourself? Honestly assess the subject's perspective in *your* world. Ask yourself, "What does this mean to me?" Then, if appropriate, tell readers your answer.

Write as if speaking to peers, not as if playing cootchy-coo with children—even if your readers *are* children. Your readers are your equals. You are doing them no special favors by committing your thoughts and findings to paper; they could accord you similar favors—they could teach you as much about their worlds as you can teach them about the worlds you as a writer live in, explore, or create. You simply have earned the right to use the print forum to reach other people. In fact, you should feel privileged that these people have found some time to spend with your writing. Don't waste any of that time.

Include words and phrasings that communicate; eschew those that tickle only you and your pride in being a writer. Also, don't distance readers with formal, uppity phrasings. This writer sees no use for the phrase *this writer*—*I* is clear enough. Wnd leave *one* out of it; talk about *you*. Extend a friendly hand and draw readers into your writing.

Write in the same language the readers read. Dropping foreign phrases indiscriminately into a manuscript is a faux pas—that's a weak joke, I know, but it makes its point in that *faux pas* is a phrase common enough to have given up its green card in favor of full citizenship. Most other foreign phrases have not. Deport them from your writing.

The same goes for dialect. Give us jes' a few words of it now, hear? A taste. No more.

Experiment for the sake of literature only with the understanding that experimental writing doesn't invite experimental reading. If your readers accept and enjoy your experiment, fine. If they don't, that's fine, too. Don't accuse the readers of failing you. You—or, more accurately, your experiment—have failed the readers. And that can be true even if your experiment, in your eyes, succeeded.

Don't deliberately try to confuse readers. For example, identify the people you're writing about, whether they're real or fictional. Don't just refer to them as *he* or *she* for three pages and figure that you are building mystery about these nameless people.

Don't take readers on a visual roller coaster ride that has them referring to chart upon chart or flipping to a glossary at the end of the book or leaping to the bottom of the page to inspect footnotes.

Play fair with readers, especially if you're writing novels or short stories. Fiction readers want to be coaxed into believing your fibs, but they don't want to be tricked. Don't pull surprises, like reluctant rabbits, out of your hat. Don't rescue the heroine with a cavalry-esque arrival of the heroic element, whatever that might be. Don't have the hero wake up to find the whole story was a dream. Those sorts of ploys aren't fibbing; they're cheating. And cheating is just plain rude.

In sum, honor your readers, your writing, your profession, and yourself by writing as honestly and as interestingly as you can. Live up to your readers' trust in you, while simultaneously making the reading experience as enjoyable and as comfortable as possible. Welcome readers into your manuscript as you would guests into your home. Entertain readers as you would friends at a party. Live up to their trust in you. Comfort them and joke with them and soothe them and make life a little easier and more enjoyable for them. And have a little fun yourself.

If you do, the readers will, like the good friends they've become, return to you again and again.

14

A Brief Word on Personal Etiquette

Upstairs, while I watch these very words slide onto my word processor screen, my wife, Sue, is varnishing a wooden toy box for our son, Chris. He just turned one, and he's napping. Yesterday was Valentine's Day, and Sue had to work at the hospital until 11:30. I had worked at this keyboard from the time Chris went to bed last night until Sue got home. Then we shared what was left of a bag of potato chips, watched a few minutes of *Rear Window* on TV, talked a little about what Chris had done that day, and went to sleep.

It snowed about five inches here in Cincinnati, and the shovel hangs untouched in the garage. When I start thinking about shoveling the driveway, I remember the other chores I should be attending to—painting the kitchen ceiling and cleaning the bathroom and fixing the light in the bedroom closet and helping Sue assemble that toy box. But I sit here, fighting my deadline and, at this moment, winning.

I should be upstairs on this Saturday, and I will be, maybe when I'm done with this chapter. I should be shoveling, and assembling, and helping that bright and cheerful young man get up from his nap and changing his diaper and chasing him around the living room so I can watch him grow up even in those few minutes because he grows so fast.

In all this talk of etiquette and courtesy, remember the courtesies that those around you deserve. Just as you should give the best of yourself to an editor, you should give the same to your family, and then some. Your family deserves more than the best of you. They deserve *you*. Your time, your attention, your love.

Yes, you must devote a lot of time to your craft, and you must take this business of writing seriously. But remember the dangers of workaholism. Remember how you might regret missing the small moments—the moment a one-year-old discovers his new toy box, for instance. And if you want to be a real pragmatist, remember that a full life of rewarding relationships feeds your writing and your creativity.

I'm not going to give you a primer on structuring your schedule so that you can efficiently mesh family time and regular work time and lawn-mowing time and mealtimes and all the rest. I'm simply going to plant the idea: show courtesy and responsibility to those around you. Give them the time they deserve, and give them the attention they deserve. When spending time with them, try to avoid being preoccupied with the words that await you at the typewriter. Granted, your success as a writer is a part of what you bring to your family. The extra income, the knowledge that writing makes you a better spouse/parent/friend because it satisfies needs within you, the pride they are so eager to invest in you—all can bring vitality to your relationships with the people you cherish.

But remember that they don't love you because you're a writer. They love *you*. My mother reads everything I write—including the computer articles I've done, and she knows nothing about computers, nor does she care. My wife thinks the fiction I write is bizarre, and tells me flat out that she wouldn't read it if I hadn't written it. But she supports me. She cheers me when I hide in the basement to write the fiction she thinks is a little weird. It's me, not my writing.

She deserves a hug, out of courtesy to our loving relationship; out of courtesy to her; out of, yes, courtesy to me. I think I'll go up now and give her one.

15

A Final Word

My last piece of advice:

Don't let all of these caveats and taboos and chidings surround you so completely that you hesitate to take a single step for fear of hearing a rule break under your foot. Conduct yourself with poise and common sense, and your chances of making a faux pas that would seriously affect your career are almost nil. Politeness, reason, and plain, simple, everyday manners and common courtesy are matters of attitude and compassion, not of strictures prescribing the placement of the pencil to the left of the plate and the notepad to the right. The rules and guidelines I've shared with you here, like all rules, are designed to help you express an attitude, a philosophy. And, like all rules, they are made to be flexed.

I like what publishing veteran William Targ wrote in a chapter of *Editors on Editing*. His advice applies to the giving of advice, but I think it applies to matters of etiquette quite nicely. "Try to be practical and understated; follow instincts, not textbooks."

And what if instincts and textbooks fail you? Turn to an infallible source. Ask the person you're dealing with:

"I have an idea for you, but I'm not sure who to send it to or the protocol of doing so; what procedure do you prefer?"

"I haven't used proofreader's symbols before, and I want to mark my galleys as clearly as possible; do you have a style sheet?"

"I wouldn't mind seeing a copy of my book's production schedule so I can see how things should be going; may I have one?"

If you're unsure about a procedure, a policy, a deadline, ask about it. If your editor or agent says something that puzzles or confuses you, ask for clarification. If you're just the curious type with a few questions about how publishing works, and you can't find the answers elsewhere, ask the editors and agents you work with.

They want you to succeed almost as much as you do.

Appendix
A Beginner's Quiz

Subtitle this section "Amateur Etiquette for Writers." This little quiz, which I've compiled in conjunction with agents and other editors, will gauge your professional image, or lack thereof, in your dealings within the publishing business. Answer honestly, and remember that if you must admit to a *yes* answer, you aren't alone. Remember, too, that all these problems are correctable:

1. Does your stationery identify you as a "Freelance Writer," in those specific words? Anyone can use such letterhead, but it seems that only beginners do. Such labeling signals insecurity. "It reminds me of the vehicles I see labeled 'Professional Ambulance,' " says one editor. "It makes me nervous." Display confidence. Let your writing tell the editor that you're a writer. Later, when you have established yourself, let your *name*, printed simply and unobtrusively at the top of the stationery, do the speaking.

2. Have you worried about whether the editor is going to steal your words—or, worse yet, have you expressed that worry to an editor? Worry first about having something worth stealing. There's a maxim in the writing business that I find all too true: "The person most worried about theft is the person least likely to have anything worth stealing."

3. Have you ever put a spot of glue between two pages to see if the editor had read the entire submission? Or have you inserted a page upside down or backward? Pressed a strand of hair between two pages? As agent Evan Marshall says, "The trick is as old as God (in fact, I believe God turned the Sixth Commandment upside-down, and stuck the Eighth and Ninth together, just to make sure

Moses had really read them) and never fails to annoy the editor who discovers it." And if the editor doesn't spring the trap, it means that he didn't get that far—which is, from the editor's standpoint and yours, just fine, because the editor doesn't *have* to go that far. He has no obligation to read each submission entirely. Remember that maybe the editor didn't get that far because you were spending time on tricks when you could have spent time improving your article.

4. Have you ever included your photo in a submission? Why? To prove that you're real? I'll take your word for it. Worse yet, have you included shots of children or pets? Our favorite photo depicted a woman holding a bedpan. It accompanied a manuscript titled "Poo on Rejections."

5. Have you ever asked for comments and criticism of your submission? Editors are not teachers. They aren't coaches. They can and do teach and coach, but they aren't obligated to. Editors will comment on a manuscript when they have a professional reason to do so—that is, when such comment might lead to making the manuscript publishable *in that magazine or at that particular book publisher*. If editors took time out to counsel every writer who requested such help, they would be fired quickly because they wouldn't have time to do their jobs, and would no longer be in a very good position to counsel you.

6. After selling a manuscript, have you asked that the editor send back the postage that was on the SASE that accompanied the original submission? That's chintzy, and implies to the editor that you think he's personally stealing the postage. (What does happen to that postage, by the way? Usually it remains attached to the SASE, which is filed with the rest of the materials related to your manuscript. There it's more or less forgotten, until it's discarded after your manuscript is published. Call it a way of subsidizing the post office.)

7. Have you ever questioned an editor about what he's done with the paper clip that went in with the submission but didn't return? Is there a paper clip shortage? Do you suspect that the editor is dealing in paper clip commodities? Can you picture editors with paper clip chains around their necks bragging to their colleagues at the local brewhouse about how many they filched?

8. Have you ever sent a manuscript to a magazine's circulation-fulfillment address? When you're checking the magazine's address on the masthead, be aware that it will have an editorial address, where the manuscript should go, and a circulation-fulfillment address, where your subscription order should go. Often, those offices are in different states.

9. Have you ever told an editor to buy your submission because _____ said it was perfect for the magazine? Fill in the blank with almost anyone short of the editor's direct supervisor: including your mother, your creative writing teacher, the leader of your writers club, a subscriber to the editor's magazine, and God. (I'm serious about that last one. Editors of inspirational magazines constantly complain about receiving so-called divinely inspired manuscripts. They may indeed be inspired, but they're still up to the editor to decide whether or not they're written well.)

10. Have you ever asked the editor to please please buy your story because the rent's due? There are many street corners where that tactic will be far more profitable.

11. Have you ever submitted a hand-written manuscript? Need I say more?

12. Have you ever submitted anything on colored paper? Here I'm talking blue or green or pink, not off-white or eggshell or a subtle beige.

13. Have you ever submitted a manuscript, only to turn around and ask for it back so you can add something that you've forgotten? Make your submission package as complete as possible before committing it to the mailbox. If you've left something out—even the SASE—resign yourself to it. Better to let the submission stand on its incomplete own than to bring your temporary scatter-mindedness to the editor's attention by bombarding him with odds and ends.

14. HAVE YOU EVER TYPED ANYTHING IN ALL CAPS? Or have you ever used an italic typeface, an Olde English typeface, or a sans serif typeface (so easy to do in these days of computers). Such type faces may look nice, but nice looks are ornamentation and no more. They have no practical value, especially if they make the text more difficult to read, edit, and typeset.

15. Do you use return address labels that have flags or smiling faces on them? Type your return address, or use pre-printed envelopes. The stickers themselves are ugly, and their ornamentation rarely has anything to do with your writing career or what you plan to write about. Similarly, have you sealed the envelope with a sticker bearing political slogans? OK, OK, I'll go along with Easter Seals without complaint, but beyond that. . . .

16. Have you ever typed a manuscript with a ribbon colored anything but black? Have you seen many books or newspapers printed in, say, blue or brown ink? Some magazines, maybe, have experimented with type of different colors, but those experiments aren't terribly readable.

17. Have you ever submitted a single-spaced manuscript? Single-spacing is accepted, even preferred, for letters because they are so brief. But with longer material, the jammed spacing wears the eyes.

18. Have you ever submitted a letter or a manuscript whose body copy was printed on a dot-matrix printer but whose return address and/or sluglines were typed on your typewriter, or hand-printed? I presume that the people who do this have a word-processing program that doesn't print sluglines (the brief lines you type at the top of each page to identify the page and the manuscript it is a part of). It's not that this looks tacky; it just looks weird.

19. Have you ever resorted to what one agent calls "Hollywood presentation"? Have you submitted manuscripts in binders, with precis and casts of characters and treatment-style summaries attached? Did you leave out the camera directions?

20. Have you ever made up an item in a checklist just so it would end on an even number? I would never do that.

Score

Give yourself one point for each yes answer—

0: Just fine

1-20: Well, you're not branded, but there *is* room for improvement)

If you have questions about professional etiquette not covered in this book, send them to *Professional Etiquette for Writers*, 9933 Alliance Rd., Cincinnati OH 45242. We'll try to answer them in future editions of this book.

Bibliography

These books will help you operate within the world of publishing more confidently and conscientiously by allowing you to understand just how that world works:

The Awful Truth About Book Publishing, John Boswell, Warner Books. The inner workings of the publishing industry.

Books: From Writer to Reader, Howard Greenfeld, Crown. A classic work explaining, with useful graphics, the steps required to convert typewritten page to printed page, with explanations of who does what and why.

The Craft of Interviewing, John Brady, Vintage/Random House. Clear, readable advice about the techniques and protocols of interviewing, from getting the interview to conducting it to following it up.

Editing for Print, Geoffrey Rogers, Writer's Digest Books. Insights into just what an editor does.

Editors on Editing: An Inside View of What Editors Really Do, revised edition, edited by Gerald Gross, Harper & Row. Editors discuss their craft: their goals, the pressures they work under, and their obligations to and relationships with authors.

How to Understand & Negotiate a Book Contract or Magazine Agreement, Richard Balkin, Writer's Digest Books. An agent explains contracts and negotiating techniques.

The Journalist's Handbook on Libel and Privacy, Barbara Dill, Free Press. Discussion of two aspects of the law that you probably won't have to worry about, but, just in case . . .

Law and the Writer, edited by Kirk Polking and Leonard S. Meranus, Writer's Digest Books. For advice on those occasions when matters of etiquette become matters of legality.

A Legal Guide for the Working Writer, Brad Bunnin and Peter Beren, Nolo Press. Information about the legal aspects of writers' relationships with editors, sources, agents, and other writers.

Literary Agents: How to Get and Work With the Right One for You, Michael Larsen, Writer's Digest Books. How to find an agent, and how to assure the two of you work smoothly together.

Magazine Editing and Production, third edition, J.W. Click and Russell N. Baird, William C. Brown Co. The textbook I cut my editing teeth on: a useful overview.

Magazine Writing: The Inside Angle, Art Spikol. Out-of-print collection of Spikol's columns for *Writer's Digest* that's worth looking up in the library for its straightforward look at how magazine editors think.

Publishers on Publishing, edited by Gerald Gross. Out of print and in many ways out of date; nonetheless, it's a useful companion to Gross's *Editors on Editing* (which was recently updated.)

The Writer's Encyclopedia, edited by Kirk Polking, Writer's Digest Books. Publishing terms and jargon and concepts, discussed and defined—in alphabetical order.

A Writer's Guide to Book Publishing, second edition, Richard Balkin, E.P. Dutton. An indispensible introduction to the business—make sure you read it.

Writer's Market, Writer's Digest Books. Annual list of where to sell your work, appended by useful articles on the business of freelancing, with a glossary of publishing terms.

Index

Acknowledgments pages, 87-88
Agents, 47
Appointments, 68, 78-80
Asimov, Isaac, 7, 94
Asking questions, 117-118
The Awful Truth About Book Publishing, 123

Baird, Russell N., 124
Balkin, Richard, 44, 91, 123, 124
Beren, Peter, 124
Blacklists, 3, 6, 104
Block, Lawrence, 104
Books: From Writer to Reader, 123
Boswell, John, 123
Bradbury, Ray, 9
Brady, John, 78, 123
Breaking off relationships, 55-56
Building good will, 55
Bunnin, Brad, 124
Business expenses, 68, 69-71, 91-92
Business lunches and entertainment, 69-71

Choosing your battles, 96-97
Click, J.W., 124
Collect calls, 65-66
Contracts, 93
Correspondence, 17-31; cover letters, 45; format, 19; envelopes, 21-24, 121; salutation in letters, 18-19, 45; SASE, 19, 21, 25-27, 46, 120; sign-off in letters, 19-20; stationery, 17-18, 21-22, 119, 121
Cover letters, 45
Craft of Interviewing, 78, 123
Criticism, accepting it, 93-94
Criticism, asking for it, 120
Crow, Elizabeth, 4, 108

Daugherty, Greg, 51, 55, 58, 90, 91
Deadlines, 44
Dedication pages, 87-88
Dill, Barbara, 123
Disagreeing with editors and agents, 89-101

Dot-matrix printing, 20, 122
Dress, 73-75, 78
Dress for Success, 75

Editing for Print, 123
Editor-writer relationships, 41-56
Editors on Editing, 44, 49, 107, 117, 123
Ellery Queen's Mystery Magazine, 13
Envelopes, 21-24, 121
"Evergreen" articles, 36-37
Expenses, 68, 69-71, 91-92

Family, courtesy to, 115-116
Favors, 48-49
Fees, 98-99, 100
Fosdick, C.J., 72-73
Friendships with editors, 49-50

Gifts, 86-87
Gilbert, Bil, 7
Gimmicks, 12-16
Going over editor's head, 99-100, 105
Gross, Gerald, 44, 123, 124

Hand-written manuscripts, 121
Heard, Alex, 95, 96
Home, calling people at, 63-65
Honesty, 16
"Hot" topics, 28, 57
How to Understand & Negotiate a Book Contract or Magazine Agreement, 91, 123
Humor, 16, 95

Informing and updating editors, 53-55, 66
Insults, 95-96, 100, 104-105
Interview subjects' right to silence, 82-83
Interviews, 68, 78-84

Jargon, 44, 82
Journalist's Handbook on Libel and Privacy, 123

Kill fees, 6-7
King, Stephen, 54

Larsen, Michael, 124
Law and the Writer, 124
Legal Guide for the Working Writer, 124
Legal measures, 100
Listening, 4, 81, 94
Literary Market Place, 56
Long-distance calls, 59-60
Lore, Elana, 13

Maass, Don, 14
Mad magazine, 33
Magazine Editing and Production, 124
Magazine Writing: The Inside Angle, 124
Mailing manuscripts, 23-24, 120
Manuscript preparation guidelines, 20-21, 121-122
Marek, Richard, 107
Marshall, Evan, 64, 70, 71, 108, 119
Meeting editors and information sources, 67-76
Meranus, Leonard S., 124
Mistakes, 98
Molloy, John, 74
Multiple submissions, 16, 27-30

Negotiations, 89-101
Newhart, Bob, 11-12
Norville, Barbara, 15

Off-the-record comments, 82

Parents, 4, 108
Pay on acceptance, 37
Pay on publication, 37
Perrin, Tim, 9
Personal habits, 75-76
Phone etiquette, 57-66
Phone messages, 62-63
Phone queries, 57-59
Placing blame, 98
Polking, Kirk, 44, 124
Pressure, 14-15
Protter, Susan, 13-14
Publishers on Publishing, 124

Queries/query letters, 15-16, 30-31, 53, 57, 58-59; phone queries, 57-59

Readers, respect for, 111-114

Refreshing editors' memories, 50-51
Rejection, 103-109
Research, 81
Resubmitting a manuscript, 106-107
Retyping manuscripts, 51-52
Rogers, Geoffrey, 123
Rudd, Sharon, 8

Sales tactics, 16
Salutation in letters, 18-19, 45
SASE, 19, 21, 25-27, 46, 120
Sawyer, Diane, 74
Saying "I'm sorry," 88, 96
Saying "Please," 85
Saying "Thank you," 85-88
Schedules, 35-38
Showing manuscripts to sources, 83-84
Sign-off in letters, 19-20
Simultaneous submissions, 16, 27-30
60 Minutes, 74, 82
Slant of articles, 92-93
"Slush pile," 47
Sources, courtesy to, 73-74, 77-84
Spikol, Art, 82, 124
Stationery, 17-18, 21-22, 119, 121
Sterling Lord Agency, 64
Sticking to your guns, 95, 100
Submitting ideas, 52-53, 67-73
Submitting ideas in person, 67-71, 72-73
Sylvia Porter's Personal Finance Magazine, 13, 51, 55, 58, 90

Targ, William, 117
Targeting markets, 13
Threats, 8, 107

Vaughn, Samuel S., 9
"Verbal jousting," 95-96, 100

Wade, James, 107
Waiting for editorial replies, 34-35, 65, 106
Writer's Digest, 3, 7, 8, 9-10, 17-18, 29, 35-36, 52, 54, 63, 72-73, 82, 97, 103, 108
Writer's Digest Books, 87
Writer's Encyclopedia, 44, 124
Writer's Guide to Book Publishing, 44, 124
Writer's Market, 26, 28, 44, 124
Writers conferences, 71-73, 75

About the Author

William Brohaugh has been editing *Writer's Digest* magazine since 1982. Before joining the *WD* staff, he worked in other departments in *WD's* parent company, F&W Publishing. He has edited *Writer's Market*, and has also edited *Photographer's Market*, *Songwriter's Market*, and *The Writer's Resource Guide*. Bill is himself a freelance writer, and he has written more than sixty published articles. He often speaks at writers conferences.

Other Books of Interest

General Writing Books

Beginning Writer's Answer Book, edited by Polking and Bloss $14.95
Getting the Words Right: How to Revise, Edit and Rewrite, by Theodore A. Rees Cheney $13.95
How to Become a Bestselling Author, by Stan Corwin $14.95
How to Get Started in Writing, by Peggy Teeters (paper) $8.95
How to Write a Book Proposal, by Michael Larsen $9.95
How to Write While You Sleep, by Elizabeth Ross $12.95
If I Can Write, You Can Write, by Charlie Shedd $12.95
International Writers' & Artists' Yearbook (paper) $12.95
Law & the Writer, edited by Polking & Meranus (paper) $10.95
Knowing Where to Look: The Ultimate Guide to Research, by Lois Horowitz $16.95
Make Every Word Count, by Gary Provost (paper) $7.95
Pinckert's Practical Grammar, by Robert C. Pinckert $12.95
Teach Yourself to Write, by Evelyn Stenbock (paper) $9.95
The 29 Most Common Writing Mistakes & How to Avoid Them, by Judy Delton $9.95
Writer's Block & How to Use It, by Victoria Nelson $12.95
Writer's Guide to Research, by Lois Horowitz $9.95
Writer's Market, edited by Becky Williams $21.95
Writer's Resource Guide, edited by Bernadine Clark $16.95
Writing for the Joy of It, by Leonard Knott $11.95
Writing From the Inside Out, by Charlotte Edwards (paper) $9.95

Magazine/News Writing

Basic Magazine Writing, by Barbara Kevles $16.95
How to Sell Every Magazine Article You Write, by Lisa Collier Cool $14.95
How to Write & Sell the 8 Easiest Article Types, by Helene Schellenberg Barnhart $14.95
Writing Nonfiction that Sells, by Samm Sinclair Baker $14.95

Fiction Writing

Creating Short Fiction, by Damon Knight (paper) $8.95
Fiction Writer's Help Book, by Maxine Rock $12.95
Fiction Writer's Market, edited by Jean Fredette $18.95
Handbook of Short Story Writing, by Dickson and Smythe (paper) $8.95
How to Write & Sell Your First Novel, by Oscar Collier with Frances Spatz Leighton $14.95
How to Write Short Stories that Sell, by Louise Boggess (paper) $7.95
One Way to Write Your Novel, by Dick Perry (paper) $6.95
Storycrafting, by Paul Darcy Boles $14.95
Writing Romance Fiction—For Love And Money, by Helene Schellenberg Barnhart $14.95
Writing the Novel: From Plot to Print, by Lawrence Block (paper) $8.95

Special Interest Writing Books

Complete Book of Scriptwriting, by J. Michael Straczynski $14.95
The Complete Guide to Writing Software User Manuals, by Brad M. McGehee (paper) $14.95
The Craft of Comedy Writing, by Sol Saks $14.95
The Craft of Lyric Writing, by Sheila Davis $18.95
Guide to Greeting Card Writing, edited by Larry Sandman (paper) $8.95
How to Make Money Writing About Fitness & Health, by Celia & Thomas Scully $16.95
How to Make Money Writing Fillers, by Connie Emerson (paper) $8.95

How to Write a Cookbook and Get It Published, by Sara Pitzer $15.95
How to Write a Play, by Raymond Hull $13.95
How to Write and Sell Your Personal Experiences, by Lois Duncan (paper) $9.95
How to Write and Sell (Your Sense of) Humor, by Gene Perret (paper) $9.95
How to Write "How-To" Books and Articles, by Raymond Hull (paper) $8.95
How to Write the Story of Your Life, by Frank P. Thomas $12.95
How You Can Make $50,000 a Year as a Nature Photojournalist, by Bill Thomas (paper) $17.95
Mystery Writer's Handbook, by The Mystery Writers of America (paper) $8.95
Nonfiction for Children: How to Write It, How to Sell It, by Ellen E.M. Roberts $16.95
On Being a Poet, by Judson Jerome $14.95
The Poet's Handbook, by Judson Jerome (paper) $8.95
Poet's Market, by Judson Jerome $16.95
Sell Copy, by Webster Kuswa $11.95
Successful Outdoor Writing, by Jack Samson $11.95
Travel Writer's Handbook, by Louise Zobel (paper) $9.95
TV Scriptwriter's Handbook, by Alfred Brenner (paper) $9.95
Writing After 50, by Leonard L. Knott $12.95
Writing and Selling Science Fiction, by Science Fiction Writers of America (paper) $7.95
Writing for Children & Teenagers, by Lee Wyndham (paper) $9.95
Writing for the Soaps, by Jean Rouverol $14.95
Writing the Modern Mystery, by Barbara Norville $15.95
Writing to Inspire, by Gentz, Roddy, et al $14.95

The Writing Business

Complete Guide to Self-Publishing, by Tom & Marilyn Ross $19.95
Complete Handbook for Freelance Writers, by Kay Cassill $14.95
Editing for Print, by Geoffrey Rogers $14.95
Freelance Jobs for Writers, edited by Kirk Polking (paper) $8.95
How to Bulletproof Your Manuscript, by Bruce Henderson $9.95
How to Get Your Book Published, by Herbert W. Bell $15.95
How to Understand and Negotiate a Book Contract or Magazine Agreement, by Richard Balkin $11.95
How You Can Make $20,000 a Year Writing, by Nancy Hanson (paper) $6.95
Literary Agents: How to Get & Work with the Right One for You, by Michael Larsen $9.95
Professional Etiquette for Writers, by William Brohaugh $9.95

To order directly from the publisher, include $2.00 postage and handling for 1 book and 50¢ for each additional book. Allow 30 days for delivery.

Writer's Digest Books, Department B
9933 Alliance Road, Cincinnati OH 45242
Prices subject to change without notice.